Seeing Things Differently

Rethinking the Ways of the World

Peter Mulraney

Copyright © 2023 by Peter Mulraney

All rights reserved.

No part of this book may be reproduced in any form or by any electronic or mechanical means, including information storage and retrieval systems, without written permission from the author, except for the use of brief quotations in a book review.

ISBN: 978-0-6458829-5-7

Cover image from photo by Lili Kovac on Unsplash used under Unsplash licence.

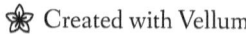 Created with Vellum

This one is for all those people across the years who have engaged with me in attempts to 'solve the problems of the world'.

Contents

Foreword ... vii

Personal Growth
Changing your perspective ... 3
How big is your world? ... 5
Critical thinking ... 8
A question of permission ... 12
What if I'm wrong? ... 15
Obscurity ... 19
Forces of evil ... 23
The world is as the world is ... 25
Forget about listening to Rich Dad ... 29
Creative retirement ... 35
Discovery ... 39
We need to talk about death and dying ... 41

Environmental Issues
Good ancestors listen to the science ... 47
What is wrong with us? ... 50
We use stories to explain reality ... 53
What if climate change is here to stay? ... 57
A new world is coming ... 60
Responding to an inconvenient truth ... 63

Lessons from the Pandemic
So, who's important now? ... 69
Easter 2020 ... 72
Updating your bullshit detector ... 74
Are we a society or an economy? ... 78

The problem is deeper than the pandemic or climate change	84
These are instructive times. Are you paying attention?	89

Political Awareness

A question of context	95
Creating local awareness of global issues	98
It's time we created an aware society	102
Drugs. We're doing it all wrong	107
We are all in this together	111
We're on the highway to Hell	115
A world of lies	118
Representative democracy	122
What are we doing?	126
Trust without accountability	130
What's in a word?	134
The one-way transfer of wealth	137
Changing the 10:90 world we live in	142
Normal is the problem	145
Disarming the police	148
Transformation - not destruction	151
We are not a society of entrepreneurs	156
Transparency brings everything into the light of day	160
A note from Peter	163
Also by Peter Mulraney	165

Foreword

I'm a crime writing, modern-day mystic with an interest in personal growth, social justice and current affairs.

It's one thing to have an interest in a topic as a reader, and for most of my seventy years on the planet that's how I engaged with my interests. I read other people's articles and books on the state of affairs and talked about them with friends and associates as we 'shot the breeze' and tried to solve the problems of the world.

Being interested in current affairs - what's going on in the world - is something I picked up from my father, when most of the news about such things came via newspapers and the radio. It's an interest I share with several of my siblings, and we still set out to solve the problems of the world, or at least talk about them, whenever we get together.

If you read any of the books I've written from the perspective of a modern-day mystic, you'll discover I've been interested in personal growth ever since I started asking questions about

Foreword

the meaning of life and why we're here when I was in my mid-thirties - and that's a never ending story.

About ten years ago, I started writing articles about spirituality, personal growth, and the skills I'd acquired over forty years in the workplace and published them on my blog at petermulraney.com. Those articles evolved into two books: *A Question of Perspective* and *Sharing the Journey*.

Around five years ago, I discovered Medium.com and started writing articles about social justice and current affairs as well.

Over those five years, there have been ample opportunities for writers like me to voice our concerns about the way things are in the world.

If you've paid any attention to the news or social media over that same time frame you'll know there's a lot of misinformation out there, not just about climate change and vaccines, but about the world of politics and power, and the rules of the game called life that we're all playing together.

This book is a curated collection of articles, originally published on Medium, grouped under four main themes:

- Personal growth
- Environmental issues
- Lessons from the pandemic
- Political awareness

In these articles I haven't set out to solve the problems of the world. None of us can actually do that, that's a collective

Foreword

task. Rather, my intention is to raise awareness and to invite you to rethink the ways of the world.

Peter Mulraney

Adelaide 2023

Personal Growth

Personal growth is not about becoming a better person; it's about becoming more aware of who you are and what you believe about what's going on in the world around you.

It leads to personal transformation, but only when you come to understand that the secret to change is changing your mind, and the secret to control is taking responsibility for how you live your life.

Changing your perspective

Seeing things differently.

If you're anything like me, you spend too much time online trying to keep up with what's going on in the world. Trouble is, though, the media is full of depressing news stories: war, political conflict, violence, homelessness, the climate crisis, the cost of living crisis, and so much more that it's too distressing to list.

If we want to feel good about life, we need to get away from all those depressing news stories. We need to do something about where we place our attention.

A strategy I've found helpful is shifting your attention away from all those depressing news stories to focus on what's going on in your life. Every time I make the shift, I notice life's pretty good where I am.

At the time of writing, we're enjoying a mild summer here on the Australian coast. There are no wars, floods, wildfires or gun violence raging in our neighbourhood. We have access to sufficient resources to enjoy a comfortable lifestyle with family and friends. In fact, the biggest challenge I'm facing is losing those extra kilos I put on over the festive season.

Thinking about what's going on in my life is a lot less stressful than worrying about what's going on in Ukraine or China, for example. It might be fun reading about the antics of the US Congress or the ongoing investigations into Trump, but it's not uplifting. In fact, it's downright depressing.

Choosing to notice what's going on in your life is choosing to be in the present moment, that is, choosing to have your mind and body in the same place at the same time.

When you focus your attention on events in faraway places your mind is not where your body is, and you risk depressing yourself with stories about things you have no influence over. You also risk missing out on what's going on right in front of you with the people around you.

I'm not advocating giving up your interest in world affairs. There are good reasons for being informed, but there are also good reasons for tapping into what life is actually like for you right where you are. You might not be able to influence events in faraway places but you can influence things where you are, provided you're paying attention to what's going on around you.

How you see things is a question of perspective. Changing your perspective allows you to see things differently, and gain a greater understanding of the world in which we live.

How big is your world?

It's probably smaller than you think.

Let's start with geography. How far have you moved from your childhood home? What do you think it says about your life experience if you haven't moved away from the town or city where you were born?

Limited is one word that comes to mind.

When you stay close to home, you tend to be surrounded by people just like you. People who think the way you do. If you have lived in a small community all your life, you probably know a lot of your neighbours. You might even be working with the same people you went to school with. There is nothing wrong with that, but limited opportunity often means limited thinking. Not always, but more often than not.

The fact that cities have more people in them allows you the opportunity to increase the size of your world. But if you have lived in the same city all your life, that is not a guarantee you have created a bigger world for yourself than someone living in a small village. Even in a big city you can still be living in a village.

I remember that being one of the things I noticed when I was living in Manhattan. And, by the way, I was not born there. I was born a long way from there in rural Australia.

Some of us are brave enough to experience living in another country for study or work. Some of us migrate and make the change of residence permanent. Others try to get an insight into how others live through travel.

Have you done any of those things?

Your personal geography can be limiting on your life experience. If you stay with the familiar, you miss out on the exotic, and that limits your understanding of the world and your exposure to other ways of thinking and doing things. One way of expanding your world is to move away from home.

Now, let's turn our attention to who you listen to.

If you always listen to the same voices it's not easy to grow or expand your worldview. Just as living with the same people all the time has the potential to limit your thinking, listening to the same voices from your favorite media outlets is a form of self-indoctrination.

You're not going to gain an appreciation of how others see the world if you never listen to them or discuss ideas with them.

Seeing Things Differently

If you want to expand the size of your world and your worldview, you need to get out more. You need to get out of your comfort zone and experience how other people live.

Change the channel every now and then. It won't kill you, and you might just learn something about the world you live in.

Critical thinking

An essential skill in the age of disinformation.

The dictionary defines critical thinking as the objective analysis and evaluation of an issue in order to form a judgement.

Critical thinking is a skill that allows you to scrutinize the validity of other people's opinions - especially those opinions masquerading as facts.

Developing critical thinking skills is how you learn to think for yourself, instead of relying on the authority of others.

Critical thinkers analyze claims and allegations in context. They ask questions like:

- Is this coming from an information source I trust?
- What's their level of authority or expertise in this field?
- What do I know about their political and ideological agenda?

Seeing Things Differently

- What is the nature and source of the evidence supporting their claim?
- What's the level of authority of their evidence? Is it data based or opinion?
- What are others saying about the claim and who are they?
- How does what they're saying fit in with what I know about this subject?

If there is one thing the last few years have taught us, it's you can't trust a lot of sources of information on the internet. Disinformation, that is, false and deliberately misleading information, is spreading around the globe because there are forces actively working to undermine any trust we have in the voices of government and the mainstream media. Unfortunately, those forces are aided by gullible information consumers with no or poorly developed critical analysis skills, who are only too willing to share links on social media.

It's interesting to contemplate the loss of the fourth estate's credibility with a large part of its audience. Some of the damage to the mainstream media's reputation has been self-inflicted through shoddy journalism and blatant political bias. But, the loss of media credibility, at least in the eyes of those listening to conspiracy theories, has more to do with their willingness to embrace the lies of those claiming to have access to secret knowledge. In other words, to a failure by many to engage in critical thinking.

A question that bothers me: Who in their right mind could believe the QAnon conspiracies and wild predictions?

I have some first hand experience dealing with people in that space, thanks to several associates who have tried to persuade me that Q and his disciples know what's really going on in the world, which, of course, people like me, who listen to mainstream media, don't know anything about. I checked their material, they kindly sent the links, and it turned out they were not following Q directly but rather people with a social media presence explaining what Q's messages mean.

It's not just QAnon conspiracies, though. How many other things do people believe without question?

Take politics, for example. Are you questioning the narrative of the political party you're aligned with? If not, why not? Questioning politicians or government officials is not treason. It's engaging in critical thinking.

One thing we've learnt in modern times is that our political leaders don't always tell us the truth. Funny how it's investigative journalism by the mainstream media that exposes their lies, isn't it. Not hard to imagine why some politicians want us to see the mainstream media as the enemy of the people.

While I was thinking about how my associates got caught up in the QAnon world, I started to see a parallel with those of us that hold religious beliefs. Think about that for a moment.

Religious beliefs are based on sacred scriptures. Books that were supposedly written thousands of years ago by disciples of the masters. We only have other people's word for that, and the people who told us relied on the word of the people who came before them - stretching back thousands of years. Sometimes I think the act of faith called for in the world's

Seeing Things Differently

religions is not so much about faith in their teachings as it is in the integrity of the people who handed them down to us.

And, it's not only the ancient texts and the teachings derived from them that we need to examine critically. We also need to question the so-called New Age texts and the teachings derived from them as well.

With conspiracy theorists and politicians you can test their words in real time. John F Kennedy Jr is still dead, for example, and Trump lost the election, despite his claims to the contrary. Testing the validity of specific religious teachings is more of a challenge, but that doesn't mean you don't ask the questions that need to be asked.

So, if something doesn't ring true for you - whether it's a far fetched conspiracy, a claim by a politician or a religious teaching - it's probably something you need to question.

> 'The unexamined life is not worth living.' Socrates.

You might want to ask yourself about the value of unexamined beliefs, claims, and allegations.

Critical thinking is our best defence against propaganda and indoctrination. Without it, we're at the mercy of those who do not necessarily have our best interests at heart. We owe it to ourselves to be informed and to think critically.

A question of permission

Something not to be taken for granted.

In *Living An Examined Life* by Jungian analyst James Hollis, PhD, the author makes an interesting observation, about parents who grew up in earlier times than our own, in a chapter entitled: Step Out From Under The Parental Shade.

"What they learned about life, the instructions they got, usually came from their models, the exigencies of their time, minus the range of permission most of us have today to examine, compare notes, and critique everything with the latest information. Most of them walked in ignorance and fear and with inordinate pressures - all without the opportunity to express themselves that we take for granted. Their lives were often furtive, secretive, guilt ridden, and silent, for to speak of these matters was to risk large consequences. Those of other religions were suspect. Though they professed goodwill toward all, they were also afraid of otherness and clung to stereotypes and

Seeing Things Differently

traditional lines of constricted exposure and communication."

Children are subject to the modelling of their parents. There's no getting away from that reality in a society where children are raised in families. And, in those societies that employ more communal modes of child raising, children are still subject to the modelling of their carers.

This is not an earth shattering revelation, simply a statement of the way things are. What struck me about Hollis' observation about my parents' generation of parents was their enslavement to their modelling.

Parents of that generation represent parents at the end of a long line of generations that accepted what their parents and culture told them about the way life was. They came from a generation that was not encouraged to question, was, in fact, not allowed to question. They basically did what they were told by authority figures - by parents, teachers, priests, bosses and governments.

The members of my grandfather's generation obediently went off to fight and die in the Great War. My father's generation did the same during World War Two. When it was the turn of my generation, we marched in protest in the streets, objecting to being conscripted to fight in a war we wanted no part of.

I remember telling my school teacher father that the biggest mistake the authorities had made in modern times was introducing compulsory education. He argued they still had control of the curriculum and could determine the outcome. I argued they'd lose control once enough of us could read and think for ourselves, despite all their book banning and thought control. (I see there are school districts in the USA still persisting with those tactics, as if the internet didn't exist. At least in China, where they regularly employ such tactics, they also censor and restrict access to the internet.)

It was that educational opportunity that gave us *the range of permission most of us have today to examine, compare notes, and critique everything with the latest information.*

I've grown up in a world where it's okay to ask questions, where it's okay to look over the fence and find out how other people live. I was able to marry someone from a different ethnic group without being ostracised or threatened with death. I've had the opportunity to travel and explore different countries without going to a war, to dive into the texts of different religious groups without being burnt at the stake, and to live in a multicultural society.

In other words, I've enjoyed something previous generations were denied. I've had permission to explore alternatives - and, importantly, my generation gave itself that permission.

Children are still growing up under the influence of their parents and teachers but, at least in the West, they have the opportunity to take on the best of that modelling and choose how they're going to live their lives as they grow into adults.

And, that's an opportunity to fight for. Not an opportunity to take for granted, because despite my experience of the freedom it offers, not all children get that opportunity. There are still places in the world where people do not have permission to ask questions or protest. And, there will always be people who want to tell us what we can and cannot do.

What if I'm wrong?

A question for challenging your certainties.

Imagine living your entire life telling others what to believe and how to conduct themselves, in accordance with the doctrines of your religion and the ideology of your political worldview, only to find yourself on your deathbed asking: What if I'm wrong?

Don't laugh. It happens. My father, who'd lived a life of certainties, had such a moment of doubt not long before he died.

When we were growing up, he'd pontificated on the teachings of the Church with such fervour that my brothers and I called him 'Pope Patrick'. And the thing about my father, at least in his mind, was that he was always right, whether he was talking about religion or politics. But, in those last few days before he died, doubt somehow entered his thinking and he asked us: "What if I'm wrong? What if everything I believe about God isn't true?"

We couldn't give him satisfactory answers to those questions. Who could?

No doubt he got his final answers when he died - but he hasn't sent word back to any of us to let us know what they were.

To be honest, I think having your moment of doubt when you're staring at the portal of death is probably leaving it a bit late.

All of us receive a set of beliefs as we grow up in a family within the culture into which we were born. But not all of those beliefs turn out to be true or useful in the world into which we are thrust to make a life for ourselves.

We like certainty but certainty only works in stable circumstances. Our world is not stable. It's in a continual state of flux. The only constant is the fact that everything changes and the rate of that change has increased over the course of the last century. In fact, it's now changing so rapidly that most of us can't keep up no matter how many professional development courses we take.

In many areas of life we're acutely aware of change. We're always updating our devices, our wardrobes and our friends on social media. But how often do you update your beliefs or assumptions about how life works and what's going on in the world?

What do you really know about anything if you never question what others tell you is the truth? Are you, for example, still living your life according to what you were told as a child simply because you've never thought to question the beliefs of your parents' generation?

Seeing Things Differently

I believe we should question what we're being told, even if the teller insists that what they're saying is the inerrant word of God written in their holy book or because it's the belief of their political leader.

There are a lot of political lies in circulation, some so blatant it's hard to believe anyone could possibly believe them. But the MAGA phenomenon and the war in Ukraine are only two of the many examples I could cite to illustrate that some people never question the validity of what they're told.

It's not just politics. Think about what we're being told about inflation and what has to be done to suppress it. Why is it that the only thing being done is central banks increasing the price of borrowing money to suppress consumer demand, while governments take no action to address profiteering and price gouging? Is inflation really driven by an imbalance in the supply and demand equation or is it created by something else, like the power imbalance between big business and consumers? Have you even asked the question? It's obvious central bank governors have yet to wonder whether their chosen course of action is wrong.

Finally, let's consider questioning the most contentious set of beliefs: the religious. For many, these are the most challenging beliefs to question, especially if they grew up in a religiously conservative family or community.

The outcome of your questioning depends a lot on how you go about discussing your concerns with others. It doesn't pay to preach or tell others what to believe or how they should live their lives. It might be uncomfortable at times, since some people are easily offended, but it is possible to have polite conversations about your changing beliefs.

In my own case, for example, I've questioned the beliefs I grew up with and written several books about what I discovered - and my family still talk to me even though I no longer hold their traditional beliefs.

Questioning the religious beliefs and attitudes handed down to you through your family doesn't mean you're giving up your faith. In fact, it can be a way of deepening your faith, but it's a necessary step if you want to take responsibility for what you choose to believe and how you live your life.

What if I'm wrong? is a good question to ask not only about what you believe about God or the afterlife but about every belief you adhere to in your life, especially those beliefs about your self worth. And, it's not a bad question to ask about all those assumptions you make about other people.

The great thing about asking the question is that it gives you an opportunity to do some research and change your mind.

You might even find out you were right all along.

Obscurity

Is it a curse, a blessing, or an illusion?

Most of us live out our three score years and ten in obscurity. Nobody hears anything about us. Very few people even know we exist.

We go about our busy daily lives influencing those in our immediate circle of friends and family, and perhaps having a ripple effect on our wider community. But, outside that circle, nobody notices us.

We toil, raise families, support economies, fight in wars, watch sport and entertain ourselves with stories of the lives of the rich and famous. But, nobody sees us. Nobody reads the stories of our lives.

We watch life from the sidelines through the filtering lenses of the media. We don't really know what's going on and, in the main, we don't really care - unless it has a direct personal impact.

Each of us is one of billions - an insignificant swimmer in a vast sea of humanity. Apart from our loved ones, no-one cares what happens to us or whether we live or die. And, no-one notices either.

The promise of a way out of obscurity

The internet - a place where our voices could be heard - promised us a way out of obscurity. But, there are so many of us writing online that our individual voices remain obscure. We write amazing articles, publish well-crafted stories, and post our ideas on social media. But, so few people see them, let alone read them, that we remain obscure - unknown and hidden, small saplings in a vast forest of trees.

Obscurity is a great place to hide

If you want to play it safe and not rock the boat or draw attention to yourself, obscurity is a great place to hide. It's the opposite of being famous, of being a celebrity.

No-one complains about your lifestyle choices, your behaviour, or your level of wealth when nobody knows about them. And, if nobody knows about you or what you're doing, you can do whatever you like and get away with it.

Obscurity gives you the option of enjoying your life in peace. But, it also allows the privileged among us to live in ignorance of the suffering of the masses of people living in poverty and injustice.

Obscurity as a weapon

Some of us go to great lengths to create and maintain opaque barriers designed to keep our affairs obscure. We do things behind closed doors. We do things in secret in the name of national security or we claim matters discussed are subject to legal privilege or are commercial-in-confidence.

There is so much going on in our name that we know nothing about - hidden behind a wall of obscurity named national security - that we've only become aware of through leaks and the actions of whistleblowers like Edward Snowden.

And, then, there are all the shenanigans greasing the wheels of power within the world of politics we usually don't get to hear about.

A moment of transparency

But, we are having a moment of transparency, thanks to the courage of whistleblowers and the efforts of people calling out the lies told by governments and corporations.

The internet may have done little by way of lifting individuals out of obscurity, but it has provided a pathway without gatekeepers for sharing information. It's now much more difficult to keep matters hidden - everyone has a smartphone and is connected to social media. And, everyone wants their moment in the spotlight - even those committing offences in public spaces.

Then, there is our obsession with law and order, and its consequent video surveillance. Even the obscure are being recorded going about their quiet lives in public and not so public spaces. Traffic cameras, security cameras, body cameras, dashcam recorders - all windows allowing us to peer into the lives of others.

The illusion of obscurity

We are all being tracked through our mobile (cell) phones and credit cards. Even if you think you're a nobody, if you're connected to the internet, the mobile phone network, or the electronic payment system, you can be found. All your transactions can be monitored.

The success of digital marketing relies on knowing where you are, what you're interested in, and you having a social media account you access through your smartphone. And, digital marketers aren't the only ones watching. Remember Edward Snowden? His story is not unique to the USA.

You are not as obscure as you think. If you want real obscurity, you need to disconnect from the digital world.

Can't see many of us doing that anytime soon, though. Can you?

Forces of evil

The devil of self-indulgence.

Are the people performing evil acts subjecting themselves to some dark overlord or simply giving free rein to their self-centred impulses to be in charge and enrich themselves - no matter the cost others may pay?

Evil is a word we use to describe things we don't agree with or are afraid of. Look at how the Medieval Church treated wise women they didn't agree with or, more likely, feared. They called them witches and devil worshippers, and either killed or forcibly converted them. And why? Wise women practised healing arts with roots in pre-christian or pagan herbal lore. In other words, they held the keys to knowledge the Church fathers did not understand or control.

With the benefit of hindsight and higher levels of education, we can now see the evil was in the hearts of the frightened, self-righteous perpetrators of the witch-hunts.

The self-interest of a greedy few

There are lots of things going on in the world that hurt people and threaten the continuance of life on the planet. War, inequality, and climate change come to mind in naming a few of the more egregious examples.

Now, ask yourself. Are any of these situations being directed by some evil force outside our control or are they the outcomes of decisions made in the self-interest of a greedy few?

If we're honest, I think we know where evil lives, and it's not in some place called hell. It lives much closer to home than that.

Evil is a choice

There are evil forces at work in our world. We can see the evidence of their presence all around us. But, those forces have their origins in human desires - desires to control, to accumulate, to inflict pain, and to be right.

We don't need to invent a devil to explain evil. We only need to look to ourselves and our self-indulgent impulses. In other words, evil is the result of choices we make.

Of course, if we always chose to act out of love instead of fear we wouldn't need to indulge in evil acts, would we?

The world is as the world is

Peace is a state of mind, not a cessation of hostilities.

If you follow the news, you're probably a little depressed right now. There are so many stories about horrible things - mostly in the name of power and greed - going on in the world.

The media seems to have lost its way as well. So much of what is published as news is little more than opinion or propaganda. The rest is about wars, disasters, and reminders of how little we're actually doing to address the existential threats we face as a species.

Whenever I tune in to listen to the news, I find myself wondering what happened to impartial journalism. It seems every journalist is either pushing an agenda or trying to trip up some politician with gotcha questions.

I've been reading newspapers and following the news and current affairs programs since I was a schoolboy. I'm old enough to remember a time when print was still king and television was only starting to influence the way we viewed the world. I've witnessed a few changes in the ways news has been packaged for general consumption - not all of them beneficial.

These days, even outlets that were once trusted sources leave you wondering if their journalists are pushing a particular agenda, even if their editorial boards aren't. Other outlets are so obviously biased in their reporting they're no longer credible sources. I guess that's why we're reading alternative voices on platforms like Medium.

The madness that is the world is not really what I want you to think about. I want you to think about finding peace in your world, despite what's going on outside in the world.

Peace is an inside job

None of us is going to find peace in the external world for one simple reason. We don't control it. On the world stage, for example, there is nothing we can do about Donald Trump or Vladimir Putin or the forces they have unleashed. Neither can any one of us single-handedly stop global warming, plastic pollution, or political corruption.

If we're not mindful, we can easily drive ourselves insane thinking we should be doing something to save the world or fretting over every disaster we hear about. I choose not to.

My guiding principle in life is: *My Life Is My Responsibility*. That is, I believe I'm responsible for how I live my life, how I respond to events, what I choose to believe, and how I choose to behave. In short, it means I'm responsible for what's going on in my internal world, what's going on in my mind.

Seeing Things Differently

We've all heard how First Nations people consider themselves to be custodians of country or stewards of their external world. In a way, we're all stewards of the external world in both an individual and collective sense, but the outside world is not the only world.

> "Each one of us is the custodian of an inner world that we carry within us." John O'Donohue.

Each one of us is also the custodian of an inner world and we'll never know peace in our lives unless we take up the responsibility of that custodianship.

The first step in taking that responsibility is acknowledging you have an inner world. It's only then you can start disengaging from the external world to explore your inner landscape of thoughts, beliefs and emotions.

Unless you examine what's going on in your mind, and choose to exercise some conscious control over what you think and believe, you're living your life according to what others have told you or assumptions you've made based on incomplete information. Unless you examine how you operate within your inner world, you'll keep on seeing things the way you've always seen them. You'll keep believing what you were told, even if it's no longer true.

You start opening to a more peaceful future by taking the time to listen to what's going on in your mind, so you can identify the beliefs and assumptions underpinning the way you live and respond to life events.

It's as simple as sitting quietly and paying attention to what you're thinking. You might be surprised by what you tell yourself. Then, start paying attention to what you say to others and how you say it.

Those two steps will help you uncover some of your basic assumptions about life and other people.

Truth is, unless you know what you're thinking and what assumptions you're operating under you won't be able to take responsibility for your life, and the secret to having a peaceful life is taking responsibility for it.

If you want to know more about how beliefs are created and what you can do about examining your beliefs, *Liminal Thinking* by Dave Gray is a good place to start.

If you'd like to go a little deeper and ponder who's actually behind the voice in your head, check out *The Untethered Soul* by Michael Singer.

Forget about listening to Rich Dad

Poor Dad has something to teach us.

Most of us are not going to be mega rich by the time we retire. However, that doesn't mean we need to retire to a life of poverty.

In the *Rich Dad Poor Dad* books written by Robert Kiyosaki, Rich Dad is the guy who knows how to work the business and investment aspects of capitalism to build wealth using other people's money. Rich Dad is an entrepreneur. Poor Dad is the guy who takes the path of service through employment.

There's an industry promoting the idea of entrepreneurship as being the pathway to financial success. That's the Rich Dad philosophy - but it's not the only pathway to financial success.

I followed Poor Dad's philosophy of service through employment, spending forty years working in education, banking and finance, and public administration before retiring several years ago. I might not be super rich but I am financially independent. In fact, my tax free retirement income is on a par with the after tax income I earned over the last few years of employment. We live a comfortable lifestyle and enjoy some of life's luxuries, like travel. I'm what you might call a successful Poor Dad.

Secrets of the Poor Dad philosophy

Rich Dads run the business world. Poor Dads are the ones in public service. Poor Dads serve as first responders, health workers, educators, and, as 2020 revealed, the essential workers required to keep the economy going.

The main difference between Rich Dads and Poor Dads is their attitude to money. For Rich Dads, making money is their highest order priority. Poor Dads simply have a different view of money. They know it's important. They're aware you need access to money to survive in the world. But, Poor Dads have other priorities, like wanting to contribute and make a difference.

However, don't fall into the trap of believing Poor Dads don't need to know how money works, because they do. Everybody does.

The Poor Dad philosophy has three pillars:

- make yourself employable
- appreciate the job you have, and
- invest in your future

Yeah, I know. Sounds old fashioned. But there is usually a good reason why some ideas persist.

Make yourself employable

Every business and every level of government needs employees. There will always be jobs. The challenge is getting yourself a job that pays a decent living wage.

The advice from Poor Dad is to make the most of the education and training opportunities available to you and make yourself employable. And, don't stop learning once you have a job. Ongoing investment in learning is how you make yourself more valuable to employers. It's also how you open doors to other opportunities.

In my case, for example, I started teaching with a degree in biological sciences and a diploma in education, but it was the second degree in accounting I obtained while working in banking and finance that opened the door to a better paying position in public administration. And, that's not to mention all the internal courses I undertook along the way to master things like leadership, customer service, and project management.

Appreciate the job you have

It might be fashionable to hate your job but that's not a particularly useful attitude to take to work with you. I know we'd all love to be making a living doing something we enjoy or something we see as valuable. I get that, and encourage you to pursue your dreams, but it's not always possible and we often find ourselves working to pay the bills and following our passion on the side. I understand that. I did it for years, but I did it with an attitude of appreciating the job I had. I made a choice to focus on the aspects of the job I enjoyed. I decided to do the best I could in the position I was in. That way, it was easier to get up, go to work, and enjoy myself while I was there.

Poor Dads know how to make the most of the situation they find themselves in for the good of their family. And, they don't give up. They keep working on their skills and looking for a position more aligned with what they want to do or one that will more adequately reward them for their time and effort.

Poor Dads are often more available to their spouse and children, and many do things on the side. Some get involved in community organisations or local politics and develop skills that help them shine in the workplace. Some pursue hobbies, not to make money but to find a sense of fulfilment or to master a skill they can turn into a pursuit in retirement.

Invest in your future

Financial independence comes from having sufficient wealth to generate an income stream so you don't have to work. Rich Dads aim to reach that point as soon as possible. Poor Dads are okay with achieving financial independence by the time they want to retire.

Let's be clear. The Poor Dad in Kiyosaki's book is not poor in absolute terms. He's not homeless, for example. He's only poor in relation to Rich Dad. In other words, he's not mega rich but he has sufficient income to live comfortably in retirement.

The question is: How did Poor Dad achieve his level of financial independence?

He did it by investing in his future. I know this approach works because I did what Poor Dad did.

The secret to this approach is learning to live within your means and investing a portion of your income every payday into a retirement savings account - from the day you start work until the day you retire. If you think you're too young to worry about investing for your retirement, I suggest you do some research on the topic of compound interest.

In Australia, we use a retirement savings scheme known as superannuation. It's made all of us indirect owners of shares, bonds, and property trusts, and allowed people like me to achieve financial independence through making regular contributions to my superannuation account over forty years.

The other aspect of learning to live within your means is managing your spending, which is something some of the Rich Dads out there are doing their utmost to make a next-to-impossible task for many of us. In our consumer societies, there is always someone encouraging you to buy now and pay later. Poor Dad knows that's a recipe for financial disaster. His answer is budget, buy it when you can afford it, and stay away from personal and credit card debt.

There is nothing wrong with wanting to be like Rich Dad. By the same token, there is nothing wrong with being Poor Dad either.

It's not a sign of financial failure if you never get to be mega rich.

When you spend forty years or more in the workforce, financial failure is not investing to support yourself in retirement when you have the income to invest while you're working.

Creative retirement

Opportunities for third age entrepreneurs.

One of the writers I follow on Medium is John P Weiss. He and I have something in common apart from being writers. We're both retired public servants with creative interests who have launched online ventures.

We're not letting age get in the way of using the tools that allow anyone to become an entrepreneur and start a business online.

The third age of life, retirement, presents opportunities for those with creative interests to finally do something about the dreams they put on hold while they lived responsible lives and pursued careers in fields offering financial security.

In retirement, you're no longer relying on your daily activity to put food on the table. You're not required to work to survive. The money comes from your privately or publicly funded pension or social security payment every month without you having to do anything to earn it.

We're living longer

Due to advances in medical and health services, along with improvements to the general standard of living, retirement is now a significant portion of a person's lifespan - twenty to thirty years. That's a long time to be doing nothing.

I started thinking about what I'd do in retirement several years before I actually retired and decided I'd spend my retirement writing. I'd always wanted to write a book, so I started down that pathway. There were a lot of things to learn.

The biggest challenge in writing a book, though, is the actual writing of the book - and there's only one way to find out if you can do that.

The world is not like it used to be

While I was writing my first novel, the world of publishing was disrupted by the arrival of the ebook and platforms that allow authors to publish their own books and receive a greater share of the selling price than they'd receive through a standard publishing contract.

Today, writing is an entrepreneurial opportunity and no longer the lottery controlled by the big publishers that it used to be. And, the opportunity is not limited to writers. There is now an online industry of writing support services - cover design, editing, marketing and education - set up by free-lance operators to assist writers to bring their books to market.

The internet is a game changer

Those of us over forty remember the days before the internet, when the only world wide web was the one we talked about in biology classes. Before the internet, everything was local. Anything international was expensive, including postage and telephone calls.

The internet changed all that. Now, anybody, including you, can have a worldwide audience, and this change is not restricted to writing and publishing.

There are platforms facilitating the selling of physical objects like artwork and artisan goods. Or, if you have knowledge and skills to share, there are platforms supporting the delivery of online courses or face to face coaching sessions screen to screen.

Learning to use new tools

There is no truth to the belief that old dogs can't learn new tricks when it's applied to humans. I started writing my first novel when I was sixty. I knew nothing about self publishing. I knew nothing about blogging, social media or marketing. I didn't know how to format an ebook or the interior of a paperback, or how to set up a website.

But, I had access to the internet and a collaborative online network of people doing what I was doing. Now, I have a website and the software required to write and format books to industry standards. I even design my own covers - thanks to another interest I share with John P Weiss - art.

You don't have to be a writer. There are opportunities for anyone with a creative or teaching streak who is willing to spend the time learning a few new skills.

The benefit of being retired

Prior to retirement, a lot of us limit ourselves through money. We don't do things that are not going to make money. We want what we spend our time on to pay the bills, which is why a lot of us with creative gifts spend forty years doing something else before we allow ourselves to be creative.

Starting an online business based around a creative interest in retirement is different. You're not relying on the outcome for your survival, so you can make some mistakes and progress at your own pace. You don't even have to make any money - but it's great when you do.

If nothing else, spending time developing a business around your creative gifts gives you something to do - and it sure beats sitting around waiting for something to happen.

Discovery

Direct experience of reality.

For young children, life is all about discovery. Everything is a surprise. Everywhere is an adventure. No one day is like any other day. It's all new.

Wouldn't it be great if life was still like that?

The difference between how young children and adults see the world is due to thinking. Toddlers don't have the language, the words we use as symbols to describe or name, to think with. So they don't think. They experience the world directly, not indirectly through the filter of a thinking mind like adults do.

When we go to school, people tell us what our culture believes the world is supposed to be like and teachers explain all those things we think we don't understand. We go from discovery to learning about the world. We start thinking.

Once you start thinking, everything is judged and compared with past experience or cultural knowledge. Life becomes a learning experience and stops being discovery.

How do you get back to discovery and away from learning about life?

Suspend judgement, put aside what you have been taught, and allow space for new possibilities to reveal themselves. We know how to do this. We even have a term for it: beginner's mind.

When you think you know everything there is to be known about a subject and consider yourself an expert in that field, you run the risk of being blind to the blatantly obvious when things change or new evidence becomes available.

All those things you have learnt about a subject become filters through which anything new has to travel. And, when you've invested heavily in your education and your prestige as an expert, some of those filters can become very opaque.

We have some ancient folk wisdom about this very point:

> "There are none so blind as those who choose not to see."

Discovery is all about choosing to see what's really there, and not what you think is there.

Give it a go. Discard your filters and allow reality to reveal itself.

You might be surprised. Perhaps you'll even have an adventure.

We need to talk about death and dying

It's the only way to prepare for the inevitable.

If there is one thing we all know about life on earth it's that it ends in death. Every one of us knows we are going to die. The things we don't know about our inevitable death are its timing and method of execution.

Death is often a traumatic experience for those around the person dying. Often, that trauma is caused by our lack of preparation for the only known certainty of life.

Preparation

Every year we spend time preparing for that other unavoidable aspect of life: taxes. But, when was the last time you talked about death and dying with your partner and children? They're the ones who will have to deal with the reality of your death and they may end up being intimately involved in your dying. Talking about it beforehand helps everyone involved prepare for the event of your death, and it will help them cope when it occurs.

Many of us make a will. We think about the financial implications of our death. But, have you thought about what you'd like to happen or how you'd like to be treated in the event of a serious accident or terminal illness? Have you arranged for someone to make medical decisions on your behalf when you can no longer make them for yourself? Do you have any preferences for where you'd like to live when you can no longer take care of yourself or for arranging your funeral? Have you written any of this down? Have you discussed it with those who need to know?

In Australia where I live, we can document our preferences and decisions about medical treatments, living arrangements and funerals in an Advanced Care Directive.

Is there anything similar available where you live? If there is, make use of it. If there isn't, write down your wishes anyway and make sure your family members known where to find them. Talk about your wishes and the arrangements you'd like to make with them before you can't.

Timing

It doesn't matter how far you think the moment of your death may be in the future. None of us know the timing of our own death. It could be ten or fifty years away - or it could be tomorrow. If we've learnt anything from 2020, it's that none of us are immune to a sudden and unexpected departure. Death embraces the very young just as readily as the very old, and every age in between.

We're only deluding ourselves when we think we can put off any discussion of our death forever. We don't have forever in our finite lifetimes on earth.

Bringing death back out into the open

On one level, the pandemic has brought death back out into the open. The sheer number of reported deaths attributed to Covid-19 is impossible to ignore, though some have tried.

Until the advent of hospitals and aged care facilities (old folks homes), most people died at home and we couldn't avoid confronting death. That's not the case today, especially in affluent western societies where we outsource those aspects of life we don't want to deal with. But with Covid-19 making it difficult to ignore death, now's a good time to talk about it, no matter how uncomfortable that makes us feel.

If you play with any online search engine, you can find all sorts of things people admit to being afraid of when asked. The reason death and dying don't appear on those lists is not because we aren't afraid of them. Quite the opposite, in fact. Their absence is a reflection of our reluctance to talk about death.

Talking about death makes us feel uncomfortable. We do whatever we can to avoid dealing with it and, consequently, we struggle whenever someone close to us dies. Which is precisely why we need to talk about death and dying.

Death and dying

Dying is a process. Arguably it starts the moment we're born but, generally, we only perceive it when someone's death is imminent - including our own.

Our understanding of death is influenced by our understanding of who we are.

If we see ourselves as our bodies or we regard ourselves as atheists, death is a moment of annihilation - the moment we cease to exist.

If our beliefs are aligned with the teachings of the major western religions, we may approach death in trepidation of judgement and eternal damnation.

If we see ourselves as spiritual beings having a human experience, death is a portal. An entrance to a new experience.

No matter how you see death, it's an experience we will all be having this lifetime. And, although facing death can be one of our biggest fears, it need not be.

Our fear of death is rooted in the stories we tell ourselves about dying. It's not the actual dying itself that's so scary. As anyone who has been present when someone dies knows, dying is often a very peaceful experience for everyone involved. Yes, it's sad when it happens for those in attendance, but most of us slip over to the other side without screaming our heads off in fear - even the atheists.

So, stop putting it off. Make a time to talk about death and dying with those close to you while you can.

Environmental Issues

It's easy to despair at our failure to seriously tackle the causes of climate change and plastic pollution. But, it's important to keep in mind that the earth has been through climate change before, including a period of global warming at the end of the last Ice Age around 12,000 years ago. People survived. Maybe not everywhere, but in some places. Some of us will survive this time as well - even if we can't stop the changes that have already started.

Whether we survive the plastic, though, that's another story - but, it's one we can do something about if we're prepared to hold multi-national corporations to account. We had packaging before plastic came along. Maybe, it's a case of back to the future on that one.

Good ancestors listen to the science

There is still time for the boomer generation to become good ancestors.

Fortuitously, I read *The Good Ancestor: How To Think Long Term In A Short-Term World* by Roman Krznaric while I was watching a three part documentary produced by the BBC over the course of 2019-20 on Greta Thunberg.

Greta's message is: "Don't listen to me. Listen to the science."

Her point is, the science is telling us that our use of fossil fuels is driving the global warming behind the climate change which is threatening the life of every living thing on the planet. Her complaint is that the response of our politicians to what the science is telling us is little more than hollow words.*

If we're honest, it's difficult to take our political leaders seriously when they allow the continued exploitation of fossil fuel reserves and the building of new coal fired power stations, while talking about net zero emissions targets.

Targets are little more than talking points unless we take action to stop burning fossil fuels.

If we fail to take action now, scientists are telling us that we risk allowing sufficient global warming to trigger a melting of the permafrost in the northern arctic, which will result in a catastrophic release of methane into the atmosphere, which will cause more global warming through a positive feedback loop.

Greta makes a lot of people, especially world leaders, feel uncomfortable because they are not behaving like good ancestors.

According to Roman Krznaric, good ancestors think long term. They think about their descendants - their great great grandchildren - and what sort of world they are leaving for them to live in. Good ancestors think about the impact their actions have on the environment. Good ancestors want to pass on a healthy vibrant planet for their descendants to enjoy.

From the perspective of Greta's generation, we have not been good ancestors since the start of the Industrial Revolution and the rise of Global Capitalism. I agree.

And, it's not just global warming we, their ancestors, are responsible for. There's the threat of thermonuclear destruction, deforestation, desertification, pollution of earth, air and water with toxic chemicals and plastics, economic structures designed to enrich the few at the expense of the many, and the abuse of power by corrupt regimes masquerading as governments. I could go on, but I suspect you get the picture.

That's enough, as Greta says, to make anyone depressed. But, there is still time to take action to clean up our act before it's too late if we behave like good ancestors, listen to the science, and reclaim our power as citizens of the planet.

* This was particularly ironic in Australia when I originally wrote this piece. Our federal government at the time was successfully responding to the Covid pandemic because it was listening to the science, while at the same time it was mismanaging its response to climate change because it was refusing to listen to the science. Stuck in short-term thinking, it was talking about a gas led recovery from the pandemic. Fortunately, we've had an election since.

What is wrong with us?

We're on a path to destruction in the name of profit and power.

You really have to wonder what the hell is wrong with us as a species.

We're facing an existential threat to life on the planet because we are knowingly destroying the ecosystems that support all life on earth.

We're polluting the atmosphere with excess CO_2 and driving a climate change that is already having catastrophic consequences. We're polluting the earth's waterways and oceans with plastics and toxic chemicals. We're clear felling forests and degrading agricultural soils.

Millions of people live in poverty and die early deaths for want of access to food, clean water, and basic medical care in a world awash with resources.

And, what are we doing?

We're spending billions on the military so we can threaten each other with nuclear destruction.

We're spending billions on missions to send a few people to the moon and beyond to Mars - places without ecosystems that support human life.

Going to Mars is not about human survival. It's nothing more than an expensive ego trip. And, while we're being honest, what's the point of amassing a nuclear arsenal and building the hardware to deliver warheads halfway around the globe? Where's the survival value in that?

We have all the solutions we need to address the existential threats facing us. We know what to do to stop global warming. We know how to make biodegradable plastics from organic sources. We know how to treat toxic waste to render it harmless. We know about reforestation and regenerative agriculture.

But, for whatever reason, we are not embracing those solutions.

What is wrong with us?

What's the point of landing a rover on Mars if we can't control a pandemic here on earth? Or ensure that everyone has access to adequate food and clean water? Or healthcare?

How about we focus on cleaning up the mess we've made on this planet, the only one we know of that supports life, before we start trashing the near space neighbourhood?

How about we work towards peace and prosperity for all on earth instead of building armies and weapons of mass destruction?

How about we unite as one, instead of insisting on being many and divided?

It's not that hard - it only involves a change of heart

All that is required is for the privileged elites to recognise that they are both the source of the problem and the key to the solution.

Far too many are suffering because the elites want to believe they are special. They're not, and it's obvious the status quo can't continue. Something has to give. And, that something is their privilege.

Perhaps it's time for another French (Off with their heads!) style revolution.

It doesn't have to go that way, though, if those driving us towards destruction in the name of profit and power wake up to the fact that when ecosystems fail, their fate will be the same as ours.

After all, we're all living in the same ecosystem - no matter what you call your part of it.

We use stories to explain reality

But reality has a way of making itself known beyond our storytelling.

We're storytellers. We use stories to explain the origins of life whether we're scientists, priests or shamans. We tell stories to explain the world around us, to justify our behaviours and to persuade others to agree with our point of view.

We do it in our daily lives, in our relationships and with ourselves. We do it in business, politics and religion - and call it the news.

We all have dreams or embrace the dreams of our culture. We set goals and expend our lives executing action plans to manifest those dreams. We tell ourselves stories to justify exploiting others in the pursuit of our happiness or to blame them for our failures.

Some of us accumulate vast fortunes or exercise great power. Most of us live quiet lives of desperation, struggling to maintain a reasonable standard of living, while others endure extreme poverty.

But in the end, it doesn't matter what story you tell yourself about your importance or your self worth. It doesn't matter what excuses you make for being a success or a failure. In the end, we all come face to face with the same reality - death.

Death is the ultimate equalizer. It doesn't matter who you are or what you achieve in life. The outcome is the same for everyone. The illusion of your story fades into nothingness as you breathe your last and encounter the reality of death. No-one gets a free pass, and no-one gets to take anything with them - though many have tried, which is why we have so many interesting tomb items in the world's museums.

So, you wonder why we do some of the things we do while we're alive, things that create a mismatch between our stories and reality.

Climate Change Stories

Our climate change stories are a clear illustration of the mismatch between our storytelling and reality.

Scientists have been warning our political and business leaders about global warming and climate change since at least the 1970s. The science is settled and has been for some time, despite the stories of climate change deniers. The burning of fossil fuels is changing the composition of the atmosphere and raising its temperature, which is changing the climate in ways not conducive to our continued existence on the planet. But what are our leaders doing about

Seeing Things Differently

addressing the challenge created by our fossil fuel burning behaviour?

They're talking about the need to take action. At COP26, for example, our political leaders committed to a framework to achieve net zero emissions by 2050, in other words, they came up with a story to create the illusion that governments of the world are finally doing something to tackle global warming and mitigate climate change.

It's a reassuring illusion. It's changed the political fortunes of some and created opportunities for others. But, the reality is we're doing very little to reduce our use of fossil fuels. We're still developing oilfields, seeking to open new coal mines, and building new coal powered electricity generators.

Greta is right. It's all blah, blah, blah. All story and not enough real action.

The current story even has a name - Net Zero by 2050. That's another thirty years of pumping carbon dioxide and methane into the atmosphere before we stop, and Net Zero by 2050 is meant to convince us we'll be able to limit global warming to 1.5C above pre-industrial levels as per the Paris Agreement.

According to the United Nations, the earth's temperature has already increased by 1.1C since the 1880s and we are not on track to limit that increase to 1.5C as per the Paris Agreement.

But, reality can't be suppressed by stories when it comes to actual climate change. Mother Nature has a way of showing - droughts, floods, wildfires, melting glaciers, hurricanes - that destroys all the telling of our stories.

Peter Mulraney

Today, the reality of climate change is impossible to ignore. It's not something coming some time after 2050. It's here now and we're living with the consequences of our failure to take action when we were first warned.

The time for climate change storytelling has expired.

It's time to demand our leaders take real action steps towards reducing the use of fossil fuels while we still can.

Use your vote to elect politicians committed to addressing climate change.

What if climate change is here to stay?

There are lots of people making noise about climate change.

Some deny it's happening. Others protest the lack of government action to do anything about it.

What if it's happening and we can't stop it?

What do we do then?

An Australian Perspective

I live in Australia, one of the driest places on earth. It's a place where drought is part of the normal weather pattern. Yes, it does rain in Australia but not all that much, except for when a monsoon or a cyclone (hurricane) dumps copious amounts of water across the northern parts of the country where very few of us live.

At the time of writing, we have a major river system with no water in it and close to a hundred bushfires burning in three states.

Our rural or country firefighters are unpaid volunteers and the entire country has less fire bombing aircraft than California. Most years, we rent a fleet of firebombers from California to supplement our own but, this year, those aircraft are still being used in California since our fire seasons now overlap, despite us being in different hemispheres.

The United States and Australia are not the only countries grappling with these issues. The Amazon's on fire. Siberia's been on fire. Parts of Europe have been on fire. Africa is burning.

It might not be enough to go carbon neutral and reduce emissions. We might need to be a bit more strategic than that.

Maybe it's time to stop spending our money on military hardware and to start thinking about where our drinking water will come from if it doesn't rain. Or about the water we use to grow food crops through irrigation.

Instead of building submarines or fighter jets, perhaps we should be building solar or wind powered desalination plants.

We've got one in my state, and we've recently switched it on to generate the water we'd usually take from the river for use in the homes and businesses in the city over summer—so the water in the river can be used for agricultural purposes.

Desalination plants are not cheap but there's plenty of water in the oceans. In fact, the oceans are the water sinks of the planet—every river and stormwater drain empties into the ocean. Remember the water cycle diagram from school?

The climate's changing, so should we

You can't make drinking water for a city or water for agricultural purposes with a billion dollar submarine. But, you can build and operate a desalination plant to produce a hundred gigalitres of water each year for the cost of building a submarine.

It would make sense to me if we increased the size of our fire bombing fleet, so we can more effectively fight bushfires, and forgot about the fancy F-35s we have on order.

In Australia, as we rebuild after this fire season's devastation, we'll need to think about the type of houses we build and how we integrate them into our flammable landscape.

People living in places prone to fire may need to give up some freedoms around house design to increase their survival chances when the next bushfire comes through.

Mind you, I have little confidence our government has the political courage to do anything remotely sensible until it's too late.

In fact, it may already be too late; and our only sensible option is to prepare to live with a changing climate.

A new world is coming

It may already be here.

The world is not the earth. The world is a geo-political construct. An abstraction. A fiction. It's a story rooted in economic and political ideologies that we use to explain our circumstances. It's a story we have mistaken for reality.

There are several versions of the world story, each steeped in a political ideology with its own economic theme. Whether you're aware of it or not, how you see the world depends on which story you're embedded in, and that's determined by where you were born.

If you live in China, for example, you see a world vastly different to the one seen by someone living in Europe or the USA. And, of course, the reverse is true, even though the people in all three places live within the biosphere of the same planet - the place we call earth.

The problem with all world stories is they are divorced from the reality of how life works on the planet. Our world stories

Seeing Things Differently

are about us and how we see ourselves as the most important species on the planet, but they ignore the role of nature in the way life actually works on earth.

In our arrogance, we have come to believe we make the rules and the earth is here to serve our desires. We've convinced ourselves we have the right to exploit the earth's resources without consequence.

But nature plays by the rules that actually govern life on the planet and it's not waiting for our leaders to get their world stories aligned with reality.

What we're calling climate change is nature's response to the ever increasing amount of greenhouse gases in the atmosphere.

Science has been warning us since the 1970s that this was going to happen unless we reduced our dependence on fossil fuels. We didn't listen. We didn't act soon enough. Now, we're suffering the consequences.

The average global temperature has only risen by around one degree Celsius and we're already experiencing more floods, fires and droughts.

And what are our leaders doing? Playing yesterday's games of geo-politics, protecting their interests, making hollow promises, and waging war.

The earth will survive. It doesn't need us. But your world, your way of life, no matter what world story you believe - that's a different story.

Some of us will survive. Some of us won't. That's the way it is.

Better hope you're living in a place on the planet where the climate doesn't change, to such an extent that human life will no longer be possible in your location, before we wake up to what we're doing to ourselves in the name of profit.

The time for action was yesterday. So, why do we keep voting for the same do nothing politicians?

You've heard that the definition of insanity is continuing to do the same things and expecting a different outcome, haven't you?

So, as a species, are we insane? Or are we just too comfortable in our air-conditioned dwellings to give a shit about what's happening outside?

You tell me, because I no longer have any answers that make sense to me.

Responding to an inconvenient truth

All truths are inconvenient for some but some truths are inconvenient for all.

The impact of single-use plastic products on the marine environment is an inconvenient truth for all of us.

We can feel good about recent moves announced by the English monarch and the BBC, sparked by David Attenborough's documentary Blue Planet II, to ban single-use plastic products in their domains. They are a step in the right direction.

The real test, however, comes down to what you and I do in response to the inconvenient truth exposed by Attenborough's documentary.

We have two levels of response available to us: personal use and social pressure.

I was tempted to say political pressure but that arena is polluted by industry lobbyists with deep pockets. Social pressure can be mobilised by everyday citizens, like you and me, to target specific players in both industry and politics.

Personal use

This is where the inconvenient part comes in.

Each of us is a user of single-use plastic products from cling wrap through shopping bags to plastic straws and bottles. Some of us kid ourselves that plastic cutlery, plates, and cups can be washed and used again - but how often do we do that?

The inconvenience comes from choosing to deny ourselves access to cheap and convenient products in order to help the planet.

As you ponder what you can do to reduce or eliminate your use of single-use plastic products, spend a few moments thinking about what people did before these products invaded the shelves of your local supermarket and kitchen cupboards. If you're under forty, ask your parents or grandparents - they grew up in a pre-plastic world.

I remember my mother shopping with a wicker basket and a string bag. That was in the days when the greengrocer packed your order in paper bags, the butcher wrapped the meat in paper, and liquids came in glass bottles. And, there was no cling wrap. If you wanted to store something in the refrigerator, you used a glass or china container with a lid.

I know it's possible to live without single-use plastic products. But, given the inconvenience, will you?

Social pressure

As individuals, we can choose not to buy single-use plastic products. We can choose to buy our fresh produce from outlets that do not wrap it in plastic and hand it to us in a paper bag.

But, as a collective, we can multiply our impact by acting together to persuade significant players in the supply chain to act with environmental responsibility. This is using our collective economic power to drive corporate behavioural change by pushing the cost of their actions back to them.

For example, if everybody joined in the protest action spearheaded by a group of shoppers in the UK and removed the plastic packaging from the fresh fruit and vegetables they wished to purchase before proceeding to the checkout, there is a fair chance the supermarkets would reverse their recent decision to wrap everything in plastic.

The supermarkets, no doubt, thought wrapping everything in plastic would save them money, which is why every little wrapped package has a barcode to speed up processing at the checkout or self-serve kiosk.

I suspect the practice is part of the emerging trend to reduce costs by having us process ourselves through the checkout but it comes at an environmental cost the supermarkets are passing on to us - we have to dispose of their plastic convenience.

What do you think?

Will you give up single-use plastic products?

Lessons from the Pandemic

One noticeable response to the pandemic was the explosion of disinformation on social media. A lot of voices self-proclaimed themselves to be experts - claiming to know more about infectious diseases and human immunity than recognised expert medical scientists and public health officials.

The indiscriminate spreading of obviously false information, by well-meaning and disingenuous users of social media alike, was a clear sign our efforts to teach critical thinking as a life skill have not been a widespread success.

Something else about our response to the pandemic I found instructive was its exposure of the social injustices and greed built into our economic system.

The pandemic allowed us to see who the essential workers were - and they weren't the CEOs and the professionals who could work from home.

So, who's important now?

Who do you see as the important people in your community now?

Interesting how a pandemic changes your perspective, isn't it?

As we fight to contain the spread of the virus and treat the infected, we're learning an important lesson on relative value. It seems we have a lot of things back to front.

Presidents and Prime Ministers like to think they're important, but they've just discovered they're nowhere near as important as they'd like us to believe.

In Australia, the Chief Medical Officer and his team of advisors are who we're listening to at the moment. Those listening include our Prime Minister who, at the time of writing, is doing a better job of listening and following advice than the man in the Oval Office, who still thinks it's all about him.

Outside the national leadership group, a range of people working in a variety of essential services have found themselves in the spotlight. Some for the first time.

Everyone working in the health sector, whether on the front line or in a supporting role, has become a hero. We're talking real heroes here, not pseudo heroes like sports stars or celebrities. We're talking people risking their lives to help others.

Strange how those pseudo heroes get paid a lot more than the doctors and nurses in our hospitals, isn't it? What does it tell you about our values as a society when entertainers are more highly paid than doctors, nurses, and paramedics? I think it says it's time we had a rethink about the way we pay people.

Another invisible group in the spotlight are the people working to keep everything from groceries to water, sewerage, telecommunications, public transport and electricity flowing. How often do you think of truck drivers as being essential workers? What about the people stacking the shelves in the supermarkets or those making sure you can plug in your computer and work from home?

A lot of these people are not highly paid either but many work for corporations where the executives are. But, when you take a good look, it's the people who know how the machinery works, who do the logistics, who unload the trucks and stack the shelves that are keeping things going during these times of pandemic.

Executives have a role and responsibilities, but what makes an executive worth multiple times the pay of the people doing the actual heavy lifting? And, mind you, we're not talking ten or twenty times average worker pay but hundreds of times.

There's going to be an opportunity for a serious review of the way we conduct business as we come out of this pandemic inspired economic slowdown. One of the issues that needs to be on the table is income inequality.

In a liberal democracy employing a form of free market capitalism, there are at least two ways of addressing income inequality.

One is involuntary through the taxation system. We may end up demanding this through the ballot box if nothing else happens.

The other is voluntary, where we decide to move to a form of capitalism more aligned to the interests of all stakeholders and less aligned with the maxim of increasing shareholder value at the expense of all other stakeholders. This has a name: conscious capitalism.

Both approaches support economic growth since they transfer more money into more hands.

When that happens, more people buy goods and services, and more people have a chance of enjoying the good life.

Easter 2020

The Easter season is a time of resurrection or revitalization. A time of renewal.

But, the thing with resurrections, though, is an old form must die before it can be given a new life.

What might that mean for a world caught in the grip of a global pandemic?

I don't know the answer to that question and I'm not sure anyone else does either, but I hope we allow the answer to show itself. I doubt we can simply hope for the best and then go back to the way things were after it's all over.

Perhaps what we are seeing is the death of the current world order. Scary, I know, but also exciting.

Scary, because sometimes the death of society brings revolution and chaos.

Exciting, because we have no idea what new world order will arise from this period of chaos.

Seeing Things Differently

Let's hope for a peaceful transition to a more inclusive world order - we know that's possible. Just look at what's been happening since this thing started.

While governments struggle to manage the situation and find ways to keep the economy going, we have been seeing heroism on the front lines of the pandemic and displays of love and appreciation across communities.

We have seen people reaching out to help their neighbours and elders, and reaching out to support those stranded in the economic wasteland. We have seen people finding innovative ways to create and distribute PPE. We have seen businesses put humanity before profits.

In short, we have seen an outpouring of goodwill across communities. We have seen the possibility of a different world, a world where people remember they are all in this together.

Yes, we've seen some pretty horrible behaviours as well, but let's hope they're nothing more than the last gasps of a broken system based on greed and exploitation.

One thing we can be sure of is: this too will pass. Nothing lasts forever, not even a pandemic.

The questions are: How will it end? and When? Let's hope it's by vaccine and soon.

Keep safe and imagine what the new world order could be, and then be that.

Updating your bullshit detector

The world's in the grip of the novel virus, SARS-CoV-2, causing a disease named Covid-19.

The scientific and medical experts, the ones who devote their time to studying viruses and the spread of infectious diseases, are telling us they don't fully understand it yet and their knowledge of its behaviour and our immune response to it is evolving daily.

Those same experts are telling us there is no known treatment or cure beyond isolating the infected from the rest of us, and that they are doing their best to uncover treatments and develop a vaccine.

Most of us are not scientists let alone epidemiologists, who study infectious diseases, so we need to rely on the advice of our national scientific and medical experts and hope for the best.

Seeing Things Differently

If their information was all we had to go on, I think the level of fear and hysteria would be somewhat more muted than it currently is.

I don't know what your FaceBook or Twitter feed is like but, if it's anything like mine, it contains a steady flow of dubious posts from self-proclaimed experts shared by friends and family spreading all sort of what can only be politely termed disinformation or conspiracy theories.

When you see a highly polished video masquerading as a documentary making all sorts of claims unsubstantiated by evidence, what can you do?

By nature, I'm somewhat sceptical. I have a degree in biological sciences and, although I don't work as a scientist, I appreciate the scientific process and have an understanding of human immunology. I think I'm in a position to apply a reasonable bullshit detector to whatever comes my way.

But, what can you do if you don't have my level of knowledge?

Here's what I do whenever someone sends me a post from a Dr Someone I've never heard of and who is making some sort of claim about the motives of the government or their advisors or who's telling me Bill Gates should go back to his knitting.

I run whatever they say past my bullshit filter. I listen to what they have to say and then review it in light of what I've heard from other sources and what I know about the topic. Sometimes, that's enough. Sometimes, what they're saying just doesn't make sense to me or contradicts what I know about the situation.

Then, I run a background check to see what I can find out about the person making the claims and the person or organisation that either made the video or is promoting it.

Doing that background check on all three parties is not all that difficult.

The internet that delivers all their bullshit to us also holds a repository of information about people created by others who have reviewed their work. Some of it will be opinion. Some of it will be backed up by reference to facts, but you'll find enough information to update your bullshit filter.

Most people pushing false narratives rely on you not checking their claims, but there are fact checkers everywhere these days thanks to Trump's daily litany of lies and the sheer amount of false information and fake news being spread via social media.

If you come across a pseudo documentary with an anti China message, claiming they have evidence about how the virus was made in China or escaped from a laboratory in Wuhan, for example, the questions you should ask yourself are: Who produced this video? What's their agenda? Can I confirm their claims?

The organisation behind the video may not be presenting facts you can rely on.

If the message of the video questions the legitimacy of medical or scientific experts, especially if the person speaking calls themselves Dr Somebody, you owe it to yourself to find out what sort of doctor you are dealing with, as not all doctors are equal and lots of people who call themselves doctors are neither medical doctors nor scientists, let

Seeing Things Differently

alone epidemiologists, and some of them have colourful histories you can easily look up.

Whatever you do, don't just take these people at face value. Take the initiative and give your bullshit detector a work out. You'll probably learn something while you're at it.

Are we a society or an economy?

The pandemic inspired economic lockdown has generated some unintended consequences.

For those of us who didn't have to worry about our cash flows, a lockdown was a minor social inconvenience.

For essential workers, it was basically the status quo on an economic level while often stressful, even traumatic, on an emotional level, especially for those working on the healthcare front lines.

But for those who lost their jobs or had to close their business, especially those with minimal or no cash reserves, it's been an economic and psychological challenge, despite what governments tried to do to support them financially.

For those with no money and no direct government support, it's been an unmitigated disaster. And yes, such people exist.

Migrant workers, international students, and refugees on temporary protection visas who lost their jobs, who had to

Seeing Things Differently

rely on the goodwill of community support groups, some of which received additional government funding to help meet the demand on their services, while others continued to rely on the generosity of the general public.

Even before we had contained the spread of the virus, politicians and business leaders around the world were calling for lockdown restrictions to be lifted to revitalise the economy.

This leaves me wondering whether we see ourselves as a society or an economy. It's not a valid answer to say we're both. I find myself in the camp of those thinking the economy exists to serve society and not the other way around.

An economy is basically a system for generating the goods and services the people living in a society need to survive but, in reality, it's a bit more complicated than that.

In the West, where I live, our economies are based on free market capitalism and a lot of what goes on in the name of the economy has nothing to do with generating goods or services. Much of what passes as economic activity is about making money and, in a lot of ways, the behaviour of capitalists has not changed since Marx and Engels wrote their Communist Manifesto calling for the end of capitalism and capitalists in 1848.

Don't worry, I'm not asking you to embrace their manifesto - I don't agree with their proposed solution and I am not an advocate of the one party state - even if there are similarities between the economic world they described and the economies we live in today.

However, the unintended consequences of the pandemic lockdowns have got me thinking about what we could do, as a society, to protect ourselves from the economic consequences of using the lockdown of parts of the economy as a public health measure during the next pandemic.

Three basic aspirations come to mind that we could work towards:

- access to affordable housing
- access to a secure income stream adequate to meet basic living costs whether employed or not, and
- access to universal taxpayer funded healthcare.*

*Some countries have already implemented universal taxpayer funded healthcare.

The vehicle for delivering these three aspirations is tax reform - radical tax reform. Tax reform based on the needs of society; not tax reform based on the interests of corporations or wealthy individuals.

What is needed is a tax system designed to recirculate the money being accumulated by billionaires back into society where it's needed. We might need to engineer some structural reform of the economy to enable that sort of tax reform.

As a society, we need to ask ourselves a few questions. For example:

Seeing Things Differently

- Why do we tolerate the excesses of billionaires while there are homeless people living on our streets?
- Why do we tolerate an economy structured to enrich a few at the expense of the many?
- Why do we allow landlords to charge exorbitant rents for substandard dwellings?
- Why do we deny people access to universal healthcare, treating healthcare as a privilege of the rich and not a human right?
- Why is it that some people do very little and receive millions of dollars per day while so many work all day for a pittance?
- Why do we tolerate the so called 'gig economy' that turns so many of our young people into low cost commodities in the 'just in time' supply chain of service workers?

You might be tempted to say that it's always been like that. You'd be right, because if you look back over our shared history you'll find that the only thing that has changed is the identity of the few commanding most of the wealth.

Once it was kings. Then it was those who owned the land. Now it's those who control the means of production and own the financial system.

But, that doesn't make it right or justify why we should leave it that way. We can change the way our economy is structured, and we can change the way we tax the few who hoard society's money and stop it from circulating for the benefit of the many.

I suspect we will need political reform before we'll see any of the reforms required to meet those three aspirations listed above.

A first step would be for the people to rise up and reclaim their sovereign or political power from the political elites currently running our governments.

This doesn't need to be a bloody revolution involving armed conflict, but it could go that way if political elites are not willing to reform. You only have to consider what's going on in some parts of the Middle East to be aware of that possibility.

What it will need, though, is people demanding reform of campaign finance laws to remove the influence of big money on the political process.

One way to achieve that would be to restrict the amount an individual can contribute to a political party or candidate to an amount low enough to encourage grassroots support, and to ban contributions from non-individuals that do not have a vote, for example, corporations and lobby groups.

If Bernie Sanders could raise campaign finances this way everybody can, and it would probably have the added benefit of reducing the amount of money needed to run an election. It should also force candidates to be more accountable to their electorates, and that can only be a good thing.

Another action some countries need to take to ensure representative elections is to establish independent electoral commissions to prevent the gerrymandering of electoral boundaries.

Seeing Things Differently

We need to remove all forms of political corruption if we are ever to have what Abraham Lincoln described in his Gettysburg Address as government of the people, by the people, for the people.

If we can achieve that long awaited aim, that would be one major beneficial unintended consequence of the pandemic inspired economic lockdown we could celebrate.

The problem is deeper than the pandemic or climate change

Most of us, given the daily deluge of statistics, are worrying about the spread of the Covid-19 pandemic.

After all, none of us wants to get sick, even if we stand a good chance of surviving, and we certainly don't want the guilt associated with unknowingly passing it on to a relative who subsequently dies.

Greta and her friends, me included, are still, understandably, worried about the threat of climate change. It hasn't gone away simply because we are sheltering at home and refraining from flying.

As worrying as the impacts of both the pandemic and climate change are, they are, however, only symptoms of a much deeper set of problems rooted in the way we have things set up in most societies on this planet.

Despite what economists espouse in their treatises with beautifully crafted supply and demand curves, there are more than enough resources on the planet to feed and house

Seeing Things Differently

all of us, and more than enough resources for everybody to have access to running water, electricity, sanitation, education, and health services.

But, the reality is, that even in so called rich first world countries, we still have not reached the point where everybody has access to those things, and the Covid pandemic is a glaring reminder that most people on the planet still live in unsafe and unsanitary conditions without access to basic healthcare, let alone an ICU.

Why is that? Why do we live with such inequality on a planet with abundant resources?

Some of the answer lies in the nature of our shared history but most of the answer comes from a flaw in human nature. That flaw is our tendency to act in self interest which, in the extreme, is expressed through greed and a desire to rule others.

It's interesting that the rich and powerful among us appear to be driven by a belief in scarcity, a concept which is little more than an artificial construct designed to manipulate the price of supplies found in economic treatises used to justify the workings of capitalism's free market.

Remember the one about peak oil? You know, the one about oil becoming so scarce and expensive we wouldn't be able to afford it.

Last week's news was we're having trouble finding places to store the oil pumped out of the ground since the pandemic hit. At one point, there was so much crude oil in transit its price was negative. Yeah, now that's a scarce commodity you need to hoard. Stop laughing, Greta!

Of course, the economic aspect of those extreme expressions of self interest are complicated by the actions of those who think their ideology, whether political or religious, has to be imposed on those who do not agree with them.

Those of us living in Western democracies, for example, think everybody should live in a democracy and we encourage uprisings or invade countries to impose our system.

One-party-states think their way is the best, as do theocracies claiming to govern in the name of God.

And, let's not forget those terrorist groups carrying out atrocities all over the place, including attacking unarmed women and children in maternity hospitals, in the name of whatever their cause is. How does anyone justify that? They're definitely not heroes or martyrs in my eyes.

When you look closely, you find inequality within every country, regardless of its system of government. There is always a group claiming ownership of a disproportionate share of the resources, there is always a group living in poverty, and there is always a group working faithfully within the system to improve their position in life.

It doesn't matter whether you're American, Chinese, Iranian, North Korean, or any other nationality, you have very little, if any, say in how things are divided up and allocated within your society, unless you're one of the political elite.

And, don't be fooled into thinking that the political elite is made up of the politicians you see on TV. In many cases, the real power is not in public view. The politicians are there for show, to make us think we have a say. Yes, even in the USA, where money is the currency of power and politicians do the bidding of rich donors and monied interest groups.

While you sit there wondering about your government, spare a moment for the people of Syria. It's been years since their peaceful protests calling for free and fair elections led to the start of an ongoing civil war. Why did it lead to a civil war? Simply because the ruling regime was not prepared to risk the prospect of losing the privileges of power based on control of their country's economy and the money flowing through its Treasury. They preferred to use their armed forces to suppress the protesters, who chose to fight back instead of remaining oppressed.

Think of the outcome. Hundreds of thousands killed, millions displaced, and a country in ruins. All of which could have been avoided by negotiation and free and fair elections in 2011. Think of the lunacy of the decision to bomb hospitals now that Covid-19 has arrived. Talk about totally misplaced ideas of self-interest.

It's not just Syria where regimes are doing unthinkable things to maintain control of national resources and the flow of state funds. You might have to look beyond the pandemic headlines, but news of civil unrest around the world is not hard to find.

The question is: what can we do about it?

We might not be able to do anything about what's going on in countries like Syria, but each of us can do something about what's going on in our own country.

Doing something is called political activism. It might involve protesting in the street. It might mean writing to your local member or signing a petition. It might mean joining a group of like minded individuals. It always involves voting but, most of all, it involves becoming informed.

You can't do anything about things you don't know about, and it's no longer an acceptable option to stick your head in the sand and pretend everything is just fine. That's called privilege, and you can't afford to indulge in that sort of misguided self-interest any longer.

It boils down to a fairly basic choice. Are you willing to be part of the solution, or will you remain part of the problem?

Your call.

These are instructive times. Are you paying attention?

The coronavirus is not only causing a few problems.

It's highlighting a few things I suspect a lot of us feel uncomfortable confronting.

Try these for size.

Why do we, as a society, tolerate homelessness? Why do we tolerate some individuals taking billions of dollars out of circulation while others have to live and beg in the streets - even in the richest nation on earth? I've lived in New York. I've seen them.

But the truth is, there are homeless people in every city in every country. Why is that?

Why do we pay entertainers, like footballers and movie stars, millions of dollars while paying a pittance to first responders and health workers?

Who are the important people right now? The highly paid executives or the workers growing or making stuff and delivering it to the supermarkets and hospitals?

Right now, the guy stacking the shelves in your local supermarket or the one driving the truck delivering PPE to hospitals is more important than those highly paid executives worrying about their bonuses because the market has tanked.

If you don't work in the essential industries that keep us alive, the people that do are more important than you or me at the moment. Question is, why do we pay them so little when we all depend on them? And, yes, we depend on them all the time, not just during times of crisis.

You really have to question our priorities when we allow our governments to spend more on armaments than health care.

Since 1945, people have lived with the fear of nuclear annihilation, while nations spent billions producing and stockpiling nuclear weapons no-one in their right mind is ever going to use. We have more bombs and missiles, that cost millions each, than ventilators, that cost twenty-five thousand dollars.

Why is that?

And now, we're watching health systems around the world collapse for lack of funding and adequate planning. Some of us live in countries with health systems that may cope with this pandemic, if we are able to flattened the curve through drastic social distancing measures and ramping up the supply of medical equipment. But, because of the way we have allowed the world economy to be structured, most people on the planet live in countries where health systems are basic or non-existent.

Why is that?

And why do we tolerate the price of ventilators jumping from twenty-five thousand to forty-five thousand dollars during a moment of crisis? Why do we, through our elected leaders, allow profiteering at the expense of other people's lives?

Why do we agree to go along with the agenda of politicians, who are supposed to represent our interests, but instead act in the interest of their donors and corporate patrons?

For the moment, we are in the situation we have allowed to develop. We need to live in hope that, somehow, we will get through this.

But, when this pandemic is over, we can't just go back to the way things were. We need to change the way things are in the world. We need to address the things in our societies that allow and perpetuate inequalities.

I wonder whether we're up to the task. I hope so, otherwise all the victims of Covid-19 will have died in vain. This event is a red flag. Can you see it?

I realize these may be confronting questions, but it's often during times of crisis that we get the opportunity to see what's going on.

Are you thinking about how we could be doing things differently?

If you are, don't keep your ideas to yourself. Share them with those around you. Speak up and say something. If you can, do something.

If we say nothing and do nothing, we will be here again, soon.

Political Awareness

Political awareness is how you stay abreast of what's going on in your world and develop an understanding of the dynamics at play in the politics of your nation.

Those of us living in liberal democracies have the right to vote in elections that determine who represents us in government. But, what is the value of your vote if it's uninformed or, worst still, not cast?

We owe it to ourselves, and the generations coming after us, to be informed citizens and to use the value of our votes to hold our representatives accountable at all levels of government.

If we don't, we will have no-one to blame but ourselves, if we allow the rise of authoritarian regimes simply because we were asleep or too apathetic to notice what was happening right in front of us.

A question of context

We view our lives from a number of contexts.

The world of the individual

This is the world of the ego, that part of you that thinks it is you and identifies with the body. In this world, your life starts when you're born and ends when you die. This is a world where it's all about you. You believe the universe revolves around you and all others exist to serve you.

The world of the group

This is the world of the family, clan or tribe. It's a world about us. Within this world we band together for safety and survival. We stay close to our loved ones, we work together for the survival of the group. We hold group values and conform.

In this world it is not safe to express divergent views. This is a world of compliance, where members obey their leader.

The predominant mindset is built on a combination of trust and fear—trust in each other and fear of exclusion.

The world of the nation

This is the world of belonging to a large body of people with common values. It's an expanded version of the world of the group. The leadership level is not local and power is invested in institutions and elites. This is a place of law and order, of rules about property rights and living together.

It's a world of legislation, policing and punishment. It's a world about national interest, the economy and patriotism.

For most of history, most of us have not seen beyond these three contexts.

We have viewed other individuals, groups and nations as different. This has allowed us to regard others as less than us.

We have allowed ourselves to believe that:

- it's not okay to bomb us, but it's okay for us to bomb them
- it's not okay to imprison us, but it's okay for us to imprison them
- it's not okay to refuse us humanitarian aid, but it's okay for us to refuse humanitarian aid to them.

There is a larger more inclusive context: the human race

There is only one neighbourhood and we all live in it.

Creating local awareness of global issues

Exploring the boundaries of our circles of influence.

I'd like to change the world, since there are a lot of things wrong with it - at least from my perspective.

There are days when I wonder why I bother watching or reading the international news. Sometimes, I tune in out of a sense of personal connection - I have family in the UK and friends in Italy and the USA. Being part of an international family, I tell myself it's a good idea to know what's going on in those parts of the world in case it affects people I know.

To be honest, following the news is a practice I picked up from my father, who liked to discuss world events with his friends. Growing up in the sixties, I was encouraged to read the paper, watch the nightly news and discuss what was going on in the world.

You could say I'm addicted to knowing what's going on in the world. I think a lot of us are, otherwise the news media would cease to exist. Not that knowing really makes any

Seeing Things Differently

difference, except to give me something to talk about when I catch up with my brothers.

Of course, none of us can know what's really going on in the world. It's a big place and not everything is reported. In fact, we're only ever offered a curated view of what's called news, and that curation is often biased towards a particular agenda.

In addition to the news, you need to watch documentaries and read the work of investigative journalists to get any real understanding of world events beyond the sensationalism employed by modern media, since a lot of what passes as news is only opinion or political spin - what we commonly call lies.

At least in western democracies we're offered a diversity of curated views to choose from, and that diversity allows us the possibility of developing a more informed view than those who only have access to the propaganda of state controlled media.

But, no matter where we live, what can we do about the state of world affairs? What does it matter that I know about what's going on in Myanmar, Syria, China or the USA? What's the value of all this information, if all it does is make us angry and frustrated that we can't do anything with it?

When you live under a totalitarian regime you know for a fact you can't do anything, unless you're prepared to risk life and limb - as we're seeing people do in Myanmar. In such places, your circle of influence is almost non-existent - unless you're brave and very committed.

For writers in western liberal democracies, the internet offers a platform for sharing perspectives. We can comment on issues, share information and opinions, and prompt people to think about what they read and witness as news.

But, are we changing the world? Is our awareness raising making any difference?

How many people will read this article, for example? A few hundred at most. Maybe no-one.

I'm one writer with a small circle of influence, and not everyone who reads my words will agree with what I write. Those who read what I write have their own circles of influence and, thanks to social media, can instantly share information like this article with their social networks. That pushes the boundaries of my circle of influence and makes it possible for me to reach people I don't know and who have never heard of me. But, to what end?

Perhaps my writing helps a few people become more informed. Perhaps my insights prompt a few people to question their thinking and allegiances, and maybe that's a good thing.

We all need to be informed on global issues like climate change and the destruction of biodiversity. These are issues that impact all of us, and the more we know about our local contributions to both the causes and solutions to those issues, the more likely we are to act out of self-interest.

There's an obvious course of action suggested in that last statement. If we want to change the world, there's very little point in protesting about what's going on in some country halfway across the globe. We need to bring our focus closer to home, to local issues and local initiatives.

Seeing Things Differently

We can help change the world by using our social networks to help our friends and associates become better informed on local issues - things they can do something about.

We need a global perspective on global issues but, in the end, it's local action that brings about change, and co-ordinated local action that leads to global change.

The world managed to coordinate local actions to stop the use of CFCs to close the hole in the ozone layer. Hopefully, we can do it again to address climate change and the destruction of biodiversity if enough of us become aware of these issues from a local perspective.

It's time we created an aware society

For a society to become aware, its members need to be awake.

Since the creation of society, most of us have remained blissfully unaware of what's really been going on beyond the scope of our immediate concerns.

Times have changed. It's time to wake up and find out what's going on - before it's too late.

Living unconsciously

When we don't live consciously, we're not aware of our attitudes or behaviours and the impact they have on those around us. We don't realise we are part of the problem called racism. For us, poverty is an abstraction, until it becomes our reality - and while poverty is not real to us, we don't see how our lifestyle choices contribute to its perpetuation.

When we don't ask questions and agree to go along with the way things are, we don't realise we are being played for suckers by the rich and powerful who run our societies for their benefit.

Who's in charge?

We've all heard stories of how bad things were when the world was ruled by kings. But, have you ever wondered how we got from a world controlled by kings to one where monarchs no longer hold any real power?

In the English speaking world, the transfer of power from the monarch to the people started in the 13th century with the negotiations between King John and his barons - the landowners who controlled the kingdom's wealth and supplied the manpower for its armies. The original Magna Carta signed by King John and his barons was not a great success, but it did create the first parliament, which served as an advisory body to the monarch. Over time, that parliament became the seat of government, in which the barons wielded the power and the monarch did as instructed. Despite that transfer of power, though, none of it came into the hands of ordinary people until much later.

It wasn't only in England that government was seized by the barons. Take a look at the founding fathers of your society- and they were invariably founding fathers. Note how little like you or me they were. The people that established what we now regard as representative democracies were anything but representative in neither their nature nor intent. They were the people who controlled the means of production, and they gave themselves tremendous powers in our name, even though the likes of you and I had no say in how things would work. We didn't get the vote until much later, when it was way too late to do anything much about it. Or so we were told.

By the time ordinary people, who make up most of the population, got the vote, the system was already set up to thwart our wishes. In the UK, the barons kept their hold on power through the House of Lords. In the USA, the rich and powerful kept their power through mechanisms like the Electoral College and the Senate, and by stacking the Supreme Court.

Perhaps the reason New Zealand's government seems to get things done is because their parliament has only one chamber - the House of Representatives. Think about that for a moment. In liberal democracies, this is the chamber to which we get to directly elect our representatives. In New Zealand, the executive branch of government is made up of members of the House of Representatives, that is, there are no robber barons exercising any influence through a Senate or House of Lords.

Bread and circuses

The owners of wealth learnt a long time ago, when they were controlling the affairs of state in ancient Rome, for example, that they could keep control of the levers of power by distracting the people from what was really going on by giving them bread and circuses.

They're still doing it today. They're still distracting us through mindless entertainment and sport, distributed across media they control which treat the news as entertainment and advertising as information.

Their strategies work. In fact, it's got to the point where politicians, governments and businesses lie to us and get away with it - because we've been too busy worrying about celebrities, conspiracy theories and sporting teams to notice or care. Until now.

Our wake up moment

Now we have a life-threatening pandemic on our hands, which has been so poorly managed in so many places that people we know and love have died. We've had no choice but to notice.

Clearly, something is wrong with the system when our governments let us down this badly.

It's taken the botched management of our leaders' response to a pandemic to wake us up, but where were we when they were:

- sending our children off to fight in futile wars?
- polluting our environment in the name of progress and profit?
- giving themselves massive tax cuts?
- transferring our wealth into their hands and calling it an economic stimulus?
- structuring the economy to enslave us and serve their interests?

We were asleep.

There's a lot of stuff going on that isn't right, and it will keep happening until enough of us wake up and realise what the wealthy elites in our societies are doing, and call them out.

An aware society does not get played by its elites. It demands transparency and accountability. It asks questions and demands answers. It works to change things.

Don't just read this and go back to sleep. Find out what's going on in your society and take action to help increase the awareness of those around you.

We need a grassroots revolution if we are to create an aware society. Things need to bubble up from below, because the trickle down story is a lie.

Drugs. We're doing it all wrong

We know prohibition doesn't work.

Anyone aware of the facts of the Prohibition Era knew we had no hope of winning Richard Nixon's War on Drugs as soon as he announced it; and history has borne out what Nixon chose to ignore.

The lessons of the Prohibition Era are easy to understand. When you prohibit the production, distribution, and consumption of something people want to consume, you provide an opportunity for organised crime to step in and meet that demand. In addition, you encourage the activities of corrupt officials prepared to turn a blind eye for a share of the profits, and create a far reaching law enforcement apparatus.

The US ended its War on Alcohol after only thirteen years of failure. The War on Drugs has been running longer than the War in Afghanistan. Nixon kicked it off in 1971. It's been a failure since day one, despite all the publicity given to the ever increasing number of spectacularly large drug busts.

Fear and the criminal justice system

Most of us, including our political masters, do not understand drug taking, which is why we're treating it as a criminal justice issue when it's always been a public health issue.

When we're afraid of something, we talk tough. Our politicians talk 'law and order' - as if that was the only possible response, despite all evidence to the contrary. We're not trying to treat the people caught up in drugs. We're putting our effort into suppressing drug use.

The War on Drugs has turned millions of people into criminals, incarcerated hundreds of thousands of users, and enriched the Drug Lords supplying what we've made illegal. Oh, and by the way, enriched the corporates that supply the enormous law enforcement apparatus required to sustain the war.

In the West, governments following the lead of the US have spent billions of dollars on the War on Drugs, but no-one seems to be asking the accountability questions.

Time to treat drugs as a public health issue

The first step in treating drugs as a public health issue is to decriminalise the use of all illicit drugs. It's not a crime to have a health issue. Then, we should release everyone imprisoned for drug use and treat them as people with a health problem.

Instead of continuing to spend billions on suppressing drug use, we could spend that money on treatment for users and addressing the issues that lead to drug use. Issues like mental health, poverty, unemployment, poor housing, homelessness, and lack of opportunity.

There will always be recreational drug users, just as there will always be people consuming alcohol. But, we can do for them what we do for users of alcohol: regulate production and distribution to ensure quality.

The economics of changing course

While our governments are spending billions of our taxpayer dollars on the War on Drugs, the Drug Lords are making millions of tax-free dollars from the supply of a product not subject to quality control.

That lack of quality control is why people die from drug use. It doesn't have to be this way.

The production and distribution of drugs could be licensed and regulated just as the production and distribution of alcohol and pharmaceuticals are controlled. This would bring the industry into the mainstream economy where it can be taxed. It would also allow the introduction of quality control measures to ensure users are getting what they expect over the counter at their local drugstore or pharmacy.

On the revenue side of the ledger, bringing drugs out of the black economy will generate an income stream for governments through taxation. But, there's also scope for saving on the expense side of the ledger, since decriminalising drug use should also reduce spending on law enforcement and incarceration.

The main economic benefit of treating drugs as a health issue, however, will come from renewed expenditure to address the underlying issues that make drug use attractive in the first place.

It's high time we realised the error of the War on Drugs and changed course. The cost of maintaining the status quo is not only the lives that will be lost but the opportunities not taken to do things differently.

It's never too late to change your mind in light of new information or even in light of old information remembered.

Disclaimer: I am not a user of illicit drugs or an advocate for their use. I'm simply calling for a more honest approach to what is undoubtedly a public health issue.

We are all in this together

Time to be part of the community.

Some things going on in the world are amazing to watch: manipulation of systems, exploitation of resources, the invention of enemies, power games, the proliferation of propaganda, wars, and the destruction of the natural environment. And, in case you haven't noticed, climate change.

As a species, we are living as if we have no understanding of the impact of our actions on the planet - denying and ignoring the obvious for temporary gains.

We tell each other lies to mask our real intentions. We deny or ignore the findings of science as inconvenient truths. We act as if we are the only important ones on the planet, while claiming all are equal. Our acts betray our words. We kill our brothers and sisters in the name of religion, in the name of politics, in the name of national security, and out of greed.

Deep down, if we are honest, we know that we all want the same things - a good life, to enjoy the fruits of the planet, to live in loving relationships.

But, we just can't bring ourselves to do it cooperatively. We just can't bring ourselves to share or to care about the welfare of others.

We continue to believe the lies about the scarcity of resources and survival of the fittest. Economic theory has a lot to answer for in perpetuating the fear based myth of scarcity, but that's a story for another day.

> If there is an original sin, it's the sin of pursuing self-interest at the expense of others.

Fear is the dominant force in operation in the world. It facilitates the abuse of power by the people with the guns and the media megaphones. And, it will stay that way until we act, until we call the bluff of those with the guns, of those who seize power, of those who rig elections, of those who buy politicians.

> Nothing will change unless we stand up and speak truth to power.

From my own experience, I know it's not easy speaking truth to power. It takes a lot of courage, especially if you live under an authoritarian regime.

But, most of us don't live in such places. We're not likely to be imprisoned for voicing our opinions. We might be ridiculed or trolled online but we're unlikely to be taken outside and shot. And, we want to keep it that way.

Even in democratic countries, though, it's still difficult to speak truth to power. Most of us simply get ignored when we write to our local member, the prime minister or the president. At best, you get a proforma email reply.

So, where can you speak truth to power?

In your local community. In your workplace. In your family circle. With your friends.

Speaking truth to power is simply speaking up when you hear someone say something you know is not true. If you're not sure about the truth of what they're claiming, ask them how they found out about it and why they think it is true.

Push back on social media when someone shares information you know or suspect is not true, and stop sharing posts you haven't researched yourself.

Speaking truth to power is simply not letting opinionated, self-important people get away with spouting bullshit.

Something else we can do to promote change is to act as members of a community instead of in our own selfish interest.

Start by joining a community group and listening to what people say. That's how you find out what other people think is important and how others experience life in your neighbourhood. Become involved in the life of your community.

Nothing is going to change if we all sit back and leave it to someone else. There may not be any 'someone else' in your community with your skills and knowledge or with your contacts. Yes, networks are important when things need to be changed.

Over the years, I've been involved with a school parent association, a political party, a parish pastoral council, a basketball club, two charities and several writers groups. All community based organisations working for a common good.

Nothing earth shattering, but all opportunities to work with and for my local community.

Get involved. Your community needs you. And, while you're there, don't let anyone get away with spouting bullshit.

We're on the highway to Hell

It's time to choose the path less trodden.

Readers of my mystical works will know I don't believe in hell as a place awaiting sinners in the afterlife.

But there is a hell, a place of eternal suffering. It's man-made, and it's right here on earth. And, for those with gender issues, I chose man-made deliberately because it's mostly men, humans of the male variety, who are responsible for the creation of hell on earth.

If you need a few prompts to get the idea, consider the current situation in the following list of places:

- Gaza
- Lebanon
- Syria
- Sudan
- Afghanistan
- Eritrea

All places where men with guns and a desire for power are making life miserable for millions of people.

If you're feeling smug about all those places being in some faraway country, these reminders might help you see the hell that exists a little closer to home:

- Slums
- Homelessness
- Unemployment
- Poverty

All of these things exist in rich countries - where we live. None of them happen by chance. They happen by design, and if you're wondering by whose design, look for the people who benefit from the way things are in the world. Ask yourself why so few people in your country get to be billionaires.

The system, the economy, is set up to reward those who already own most of your nation's wealth.

A few more things to think about:

- Corruption
- Crony capitalism
- Interest groups
- Propaganda

I, like most of my readers, live in a liberal democracy, where we're supposed to have representative government, meaning our elected representatives (politicians) are meant to serve the interests of their electorates, that is, us, the people. If you follow politics, you already know, with few exceptions, that's not happening anywhere.

And where is 'the way things are' taking us? Here are a couple of indicators of our destination:

- Man-made global warming driven climate change
- Destruction of the natural environment due to over exploitation of resources and unchecked pollution

In other words, a world you won't be able to live in, even if you're one of the billionaires.

You'd think, with all the reports and modelling on the current trajectory of our growth driven economic activity, our leaders would be doing more than making empty promises about addressing the issues which, if left unchecked, will lead to the destruction of all life on the planet.

My question for our leaders.

What's the point of maintaining the status quo, if it's going to lead to an uninhabitable planet?

It doesn't matter how rich you are, you can't buy your way off a dying planet - despite the current space travel antics of a few billionaires.

It's time to choose the other path, the path less trodden that leads to life and prosperity for all.

A world of lies

What happened to the simple life where there were sources of truth you could trust?

How do people arrive at the conclusion that everything reported in the mainstream media is a lie? I have a friend, for example, who not only claims there is no such thing as Covid but that there is no war going on in Ukraine. According to her, it's all American propaganda.

My friend refuses to engage with mainstream media. She gets all of her 'information' from non-mainstream media sources on the internet.

The irony is she's not prepared to believe anything written by credentialed journalists but she believes anything written or spoken by her non-mainstream media sources - people she doesn't know but who, for some reason, she has chosen to trust.

Seeing Things Differently

According to my friend, I have been brainwashed by the mainstream media. Of course, she and her group know 'the truth' about what's really going on in the world, and I don't.

Now, there's probably some truth in her claim. There are media outlets pumping out propaganda - messages designed to promote certain interests or to obscure the truth. We could all probably name one in our local market. That's why it pays to know who owns or controls particular outlets.

Unless you live in a country controlled by an authoritarian regime, in which case you probably wouldn't be reading this, you have access to a range of mainstream media sources. Not all those sources are politically aligned or controlled by the same corporate interests. It makes sense to check information through several sources and not to rely on one source alone. It also pays to apply critical thinking to your media consumption before accepting any story as fact.

In Australia, the most trusted news sources are the Australian Broadcasting Commission (ABCNews) and the Special Broadcasting Service (SBSNews), both of which are public service broadcasters primarily funded by taxpayers, which operate independent of government under the terms of legislated charters. Staffed by professional journalists, both outlets compete with commercial media for our attention across the 24 hour news cycle.

Some of our commercial news sources are editorially biased and promote particular agendas, however, they are subject to fact checking and their journalists operate under a voluntary code of ethics. The ABC even has a Media Watch program that names and shames egregious breaches of professional reporting standards.

Unregulated alternative sources

It's a big leap of faith to believe all mainstream media are lying to us about what's going on in the world. But, if you reject the mainstream as propaganda and turn to the internet for your information, what are you exposing yourself to?

The internet is mostly unregulated. Anyone can post articles, upload videos or release podcasts. The internet is like a market square where you can stand on your soap box and say whatever you want. You can dress up your opinion or fabrication as fact and release it into the wild. You can promote other people's interpretation of the facts as the truth. It's both a fun and dangerous place for anyone doing their own 'research'.

I suspect people like my friend are looking for reasons to explain why life is the way it is for them. They've been lied to by their political leaders, aided and abetted by media outlets more interested in ratings than truth, since ratings, not truth, drive the advertising dollars. So, it's little wonder some are seeking out alternative sources.

What I'd like to know, though, is why do people choose to believe the obvious lies these non-mainstream sources tell them?

How do you get sucked in by QAnon, for example?

Why would you choose to believe a celebrity over a public health official when it comes to a pandemic?

Who's doing the brainwashing? I'm not sure it's only the mainstream media.

Seeing Things Differently

The worst part is you can't have a rational discussion about any of this with someone like my friend. It's relationship ending if you voice your disagreement with their interpretation of the truth.

Maybe we really do live in a multiverse and it's only a problem when our worlds intersect, but I'm not convinced.

After all, not believing in Covid hasn't stopped anyone from dying from it as far as I know, and the production of all that footage from Ukraine must be costing someone a fortune, if it's all fake.

Representative democracy

It works when you participate.

On the 21st of May, 2022, Australians voted in a federal election and changed their government without claims of stolen votes or an insurrection.

Australia is one of 22 countries with mandatory voting for all citizens eligible to vote and generally has a voter turnout in excess of 90% for federal elections. This might have something to do with elections being held on a Saturday and postal and pre-polling day voting provisions. That's right, Australia makes it easy for people to vote.

For its House of Representatives, Australia uses a preferential voting system, which means voters are required to vote for every candidate standing in their electorate in order of preference. The candidate who achieves more than 50% of the vote based on preferences is elected.

Voting for the Senate uses a quota system based on the population of the State or Territory electing senators combined with preferential voting. Australia has a half Senate election each time there is an election for the House of Representatives, unless a legislative deadlock triggers a double dissolution election when all members of both houses must go to the people.

Federal elections are conducted by the Australian Electoral Commission (AEC) which is an impartial public service agency. The AEC is also responsible for electoral boundaries - so there is no gerrymandering either.

Australia has two main political parties

Australian politics has been dominated by two major political groups for the last fifty years or so: the Australian Labor Party (ALP) and the Liberal National Party coalition (LNP). There is a gaggle of minor parties, the largest being the Greens.

Prior to election day 2022, the LNP had been in government since the 2013 election and was hoping to extend its time in government to a fourth term. But, the LNP made the mistake of not listening to the electorate on several issues, including climate change, gender equity, accountability and the call for indigenous recognition in the constitution, so it was voted out.

Although the ALP won enough seats to have a two seat majority in the House of Representatives, it did not win all the seats the LNP, especially the Liberal Party, lost. Around half of those seats went to Independents or the Greens.

The Greens now have 4 members, up from 1, and there are 12 independents, up from 5.

This time we did something different

This time we elected community based independent candidates in what were regarded as safe Liberal Party seats, and several independent candidates were re-elected.

The difference came from the way the independent candidates were selected - their communities chose them. They were not chosen or supported by a political party. They were put forward by community based groups that morphed into their campaign teams. And, their campaigns were partially funded through crowdfunding coordinated by Climate 200.

In other words, across the country people decided to participate and elect a candidate they knew would represent them in the Parliament - and to do so in a targeted way that would hurt the government. As the result shows, it worked.

In the new Parliament the Community Independents will sit on the cross benches but the Government will ignore them at its peril.

A clear message has been sent to the major political parties: represent our interests or we will replace you with local candidates who will represent us.

The Takeaway

The people living in an electoral district can make a difference when they decide to participate in the workings of their democracy.

It's no longer safe to leave the power of government in the hands of party aligned politicians beholden to big money

Seeing Things Differently

donors. They do not represent your interests. They do not listen to you.

Things only change when voters are prepared to participate and insist on representative being the operative word in representative democracy.

What are we doing?

Some of the things we're doing are incomprehensible to the thinking mind.

Who in their right mind, for example, would start a war and then go on to destroy everything in the country they claim to be liberating? Yet, Russia is conducting such a war in Ukraine, though it's not the only war currently being waged on the planet.

As insane as that is, we also have people talking up a war between the US and China, and North Korea lobbing missiles into the Pacific, threatening to start a nuclear conflagration if South Korea doesn't acquiesce to its demands.

And, as if all the wars threatening life on the planet weren't enough, we're also experiencing an on-going stream of devastating climate-change-driven storms, floods and fires.

What is going on? Are the forces of the universe breaking everything apart to allow for the birth of the new? Maybe,

Seeing Things Differently

but I suspect most of the blame lies somewhat closer to home.

Birth and death are two aspects of the great cycle of life on this planet. Every person born, dies. Every tree that grows in the forest falls to the ground to be recycled. Civilisations do the same, the only difference being the span of time marking their existence.

We certainly seem hell-bent on bringing about our own destruction, and not only in the West.

What drives people to make short-term profit-driven decisions leading to the destruction of life on the planet when there are other options?

Don't the people running our industries realise there is only this one planet supporting life as we know it in the universe?

How wilfully ignorant do you have to be to continue activities that poison all life on the planet for the sake of making a profit?

We aren't living in an episode of Star Trek, no matter what Elon Musk, with his dreams of relocating life to Mars, may think.

Want to make money? Invest in the technologies that will enable our transition to a carbon neutral economy. How about making money from cleaning up the mess created by industry, instead of adding to it?

Want peace on the planet? Stop supporting the military industrial worldview.

Why is it that we're always building bigger and more destructive weapons, instead of engaging in dialogue and finding ways to maintain the peace?

Why do political leaders believe their nation has to dominate the world?

What ever happened to the idea of peaceful co-existence?

Why do we persist with the United Nations, if no-one takes its resolutions seriously?

It's time to remember that there is only one humanity and one Earth, and nobody gets to take anything with them when they leave the planet at death.

It doesn't matter how wealthy you become or how much power you acquire, you'll leave it all behind when your time's up and, if you don't look after the planet while you're here, your descendants won't survive no matter how much stuff you leave them.

There is still time to correct our ways, but we no longer have the luxury of that time being unlimited, if we're going to avoid the arrival of a climate not supportive of life on the planet.

Individually, most of us can't do anything to make much of a difference, but collectively we can.

Our political leaders won't change their behaviour unless we demand it or change our political leaders.

Our industrial leaders won't change their behaviour until we stop investing in their companies and buying their products.

Seeing Things Differently

Yes, George W was right. Consumers do have power and they drive the economy. Nobody makes a profit if you don't buy what they're selling.

Nobody will do anything unless we talk about the issues and point out the absurdities of our current behaviours. And, nobody will listen until we stop squabbling over insignificant things and calling each other names.

Your ideology won't matter when global temperatures rise by 3 degrees C or more, or some crazy decides nuclear war is a valid option.

We need to wake up to what we're doing. Yes, we all need to be woke - or there will be nobody here to read Roald Dahl's newly censored books to the next generation of kids.

Trust without accountability

A pathway to collapse for liberal democratic societies.

Trust is an essential ingredient of all successful relationships.

When trust is betrayed, relationships collapse. Friendships dissolve. Marriages end. Customers take their business elsewhere. Supporters abandon the team. People protest in the streets. Governments are voted out. Societies fall apart.

When everything is going well, we take trust for granted. We're unaware of the level of trust underpinning everything going on in society.

Trust in action

Consider the microchip enhanced piece of plastic you use to pay for your shopping. You tap it on the payment terminal, a few lights flash, the screen lights up with those magic words: transaction approved, and they let you take whatever you purchased out of the store.

No money has changed hands within the store. They've let you buy hundreds of dollars worth of merchandise by waving a piece of plastic at an electronic device, although they usually want you to key in your personal identification number for larger purchases.

You and the store are relying on the payment system linked to your plastic card to move money from your account to theirs. That's trust in operation at a transactional level.

The other side of a trust transaction is accountability. No merchant is going to continue allowing you to wave your piece of plastic in exchange for goods and services if the banks don't keep their side of the bargain. And, your bank will only do that for you as long as you keep putting money into the account connected to that plastic card.

We all make promises that need to be kept if the system is to stay in operation. The name given to the pieces of paper that facilitated an earlier form of cashless transactions - promissory notes - is a good reminder of what allows the system to work.

Trust beyond financial transactions

Trust and accountability aren't only essential to the operation of financial transactions. The trust - accountability nexus underpins all relationships. It underpins the very existence of liberal democratic societies.

We trust others until something breaks that trust. And, there is nothing like betrayal when it comes to breaking trust.

When your partner or child lies to you, they erode your trust. They might fool you a few times, but very few of us are fooled for long. And, think what it does to the trust you've established when you lie to your children or say one thing but do another.

Trust involves faithfulness, truthfulness, acting with integrity, and accountability from all parties to a relationship.

Political accountability

Breakdowns on the accountability side of the trust equation are cause for concern. It's devastating when betrayals of trust destroy personal relationships.

It's potentially catastrophic when those betrayals occur at the political level and our leaders think they can get away with lying to us and inventing alternative facts to suit their narrative at our expense. It's even more dangerous when they decide accountability and truth telling are no longer necessary and everything we see or hear from either a government or political party is propaganda.

For those of us watching the world of politics, it's a concern that elements of the media have joined the political propaganda machine, choosing to amplify the lies told by politicians and special interest groups instead of investigating and exposing them.

We're almost at the point of not knowing whose voice to trust or whose version of the story is about the facts and whose is nothing more than a narrative designed to confuse us.

Seeing Things Differently

It's easy to blame politicians, corrupt corporates, and biased media commentators - but they only get away with it when we abdicate our responsibilities.

If we want to continue living in a society based on trust, where nobody is above the law, where laws are equitable, and our rights are respected, we need to hold our elected leaders accountable.

We need to become informed, protest, and vote.

Silence is always mistaken as consent. We need to make noise. We need to speak up now.

It will be too late to protest after we've lost the freedom to do so.

What's in a word?

A lot when the word is woke.

Woke: (adjective) US *informal,* alert to injustice in society, especially racism.

In the rest of the world, we'd describe a person alert to the injustices in society as awake or aware, maybe we'd even go so far as to say they were informed, but Americans like to highlight their exceptionalism, even when it comes to the English language. They describe such people as woke.

Despite the obvious benefits of having an informed citizenry, woke has become a term of derision in contemporary, conservative politics. The question is: Why?

Conservatives, by definition, want to maintain the status quo. They stand for traditional social values. They're not into change or innovation. I suspect they're also into power, since they like to tell other people how to live their lives.

I have a feeling that conservatives are afraid of the woke mob, the people aware of what's going on in society.

Seeing Things Differently

The woke are the ones that see the strings being pulled by the rich and powerful, and they're the ones on the receiving end of the injustices built into the way a society operates. It's not much fun being one of the oppressed or marginalised, especially when you know it doesn't have to be that way.

This is not a uniquely American phenomenon. You only need to tune into the no campaign regarding the referendum for an indigenous voice to parliament in Australia or the suppression of women's rights in places like Iran or Afghanistan or read anything on the causes of poverty to see it's a worldwide problem.

I suspect conservatives attack those exposing what's wrong with the way their society operates because they don't want to be held accountable, and they definitely don't want to give up their positions of power and privilege.

After all, the woke are the people calling for changes to address known injustices, and those changes usually involve a redistribution of rights and resources from the rich and powerful to those currently being oppressed or exploited.

What I find interesting about resistance to the so-called woke agenda is its religious dimension, especially from Christian groups. I don't know enough about Islam to critique the Mullahs in Iran or Afghanistan, although I suspect their treatment of women has more to do with power than belief.

From my perspective as an urban mystic with a Christian background, however, it's incomprehensible how anyone who claims to be a follower of the Nazarene can knowingly participate in the continued oppression, exclusion, and exploitation of others.

Peter Mulraney

We say we have values, but are we living the values we espouse or hanging on to our positions of power and privilege?

You might want to consider what your response to social justice issues says about you and your values before you answer that question.

Whatever your answer, remember, it's never too late to change your mind or your vote.

The one-way transfer of wealth

The basic economics of inequality.

There are two groups of people operating in the economy: those that own the income producing assets and those that don't. The first group is relatively small, the so-called one percent - the wealthy. The rest of us make up the second.

The wealthy own income producing assets like businesses which sell goods and services for money, or assets like real estate or intellectual property which the rest of us pay money to use.

People who don't own income producing assets work for those that do, and then spend their wages buying the products and services they work so hard to produce or on renting assets owned by others that they can't afford to buy. In other words, the ninety-nine percent are transferring their wealth to the one percent through their daily acts of survival based consumption.

The operating rules of the economy allow money itself to be treated as an income producing asset. That's what's happening when you pay to use other people's money to purchase non-income producing items like a house or a vehicle for personal use. It's even what's behind the creation of credit cards, which are designed to encourage you to spend your wages before you earn them and then pay for the privilege.

Within the non-asset owning group is a subset of people who, for a variety of reasons, do not or cannot work for income producing asset owners. These are the people that rely on welfare, charity, or begging to survive, and are often homeless.

Government

The operation of the economy is regulated by government through the imposition of rules. This happens because history tells us the people who promote the concept of 'market forces' are not to be trusted.

A current example of an outcome attributed to 'market forces' in action is the cost of living crisis. Economists say the crisis is being driven by inflation. That inflation, however, is not being caused by upward wage pressures - because there aren't any. It's being driven by business owners using pandemic related supply chain issues and the war in Ukraine as excuses to push up prices and expand profit margins.

Some governments intervened in the market to limit the inflationary pressures created by increased energy costs, when it became obvious energy companies were price gouging - increasing their prices while their costs had not changed - at the expense of all other parts of the economy. Of course the energy producers accredited their windfall profits to the operation of 'market forces' and argued governments were stifling investment in the sector.

Unfortunately, many governments are politically timid. They're reluctant to change fiscal policy settings or introduce regulation to reduce inflationary pressures. Instead, they leave it to central banks to tame inflation.

The strategy central banks use to stop people spending on consumption, in order to reduce inflationary demand pressures, is to force borrowers to pay more for the money used to fund their home loan, personal loan or credit card debt. It's still a wealth transfer, but instead of going to the owners of retail businesses, it's now going to the owners of the retail banks.

Taxation

A primary function of government is taxation - collecting money from citizens to pay for public services.

The easiest people to tax are wage earners and governments all over the world have found efficient ways to do that. Usually, they direct your employer to withhold taxes from your wages and pass it to Treasury every time you get paid. Simple, because your wage is a known amount. Easy, because they know who employs you.

The most difficult people to collect taxes from are self-employed small business owners, because nobody outside the business really knows how much profit they make. Their tax reporting is based on trust - and the fear of being audited by the tax authorities.

The wealthy live in a different realm altogether when it comes to taxation. They reside in the world of political donations and influence, and they have history on their side. It was the wealthy who created government and wrote the rules when they took the power to rule away from monarchs.

The wealthy don't like paying tax and have gamed the system to make sure they pay as little as possible. They use tax havens to hide their wealth and have birthed an industry of tax accountants only too willing to help them avoid paying tax - for an appropriate fee.

Over the last few decades, as I'm sure you're aware, wages have stagnated. At the same time, however, the wealthy have somehow managed to get wealthier.

We are witnessing the creation of an ever-growing inequality in society, one which is being enabled by the failure of governments to adequately tax the wealthy.

Taxation rates for the wealthy became inadequate when governments embraced the discredited concept of trickle down economics, and continue to be inadequate while governments refuse to tax capital gains and investment returns at the same rate as income.

Wealth redistribution

The current flow of wealth is from wage earners to the already wealthy, while the burden of paying for public

Seeing Things Differently

services falls primarily on those same wage earners.

We are living in a world where some people are spending millions on houses in parts of the same city where, a few blocks away, homeless people are living in the streets.

We are living in a world where executives are paying themselves thousands of times the amount they pay their front line workers.

We're living in a fantasy world if we think this can continue indefinitely.

If we want our society to survive, we need to do something about wealth redistribution before our economic bubble bursts. In my opinion, there are two ways wealth can be redistributed.

One way is to introduce an effective taxation regime that transfers wealth from the already wealthy to the wider community. Such a regime would need to encourage a more equitable approach to wages and provide a greater social safety net designed to eliminate poverty.

The other way involves the violent transfer of wealth through revolution.

I know which way I'd prefer to see it happen - but I'm not the one calling the shots.

If we want a peaceful redistribution, we need to pressure our politicians to act in our common interest, and not in the interest of their current patrons.

Otherwise, it will be up to the mob - and that won't be peaceful.

Changing the 10:90 world we live in

Living in interdependent worlds with opposing priorities.

We live in a world defined by the interplay of capitalism and consumption. No matter how you look at that interplay, though, it's not happening on a level playing field.

The game is rigged in the interest of the capitalists - the 10 percent of the population that controls the wealth generating means of production and most other levers of power.

However, we're all consumers. Even the members of the 10 percent. The problem is most of us making up the 90 percent are only consumers. We own nothing of economic or wealth generating value, apart from our labour - and we need to hire ourselves out in exchange for money in order to survive as consumers.

We can summarise the interplay between our worlds like this. They control. We consume. They control the means of production. We need to make a living. They control the politicians. We vote. They control the media. We want to be informed.

The 10 percent only get away with what they're doing because we let them

Most of us don't even understand the basic rules of the game, which, I suspect, is the desired outcome. After all, one of the hallmarks of the wealthy 10 percent is they know how to hold on to their wealth and influence.

Let's get one thing clear, though. Despite our shortcomings, the 10 percent depend on the rest of us. We're the people they treat as resources when it comes to making things and providing services, and we're the people that buy the goods and services they provide.

Trouble is, though, the interplay is not a fair exchange, which is why we've seen the rise of billionaires during a period of prolonged wage stagnation. The benefits of the last twenty years or so of increased productivity are clearly flowing one way - and, it's not to us.

Clearly, the current arrangements are not a level playing field - it's tilted in favour of the 10 percent. Obviously, if things are to change, the impetus is not going to come from the 10 percent. It's going to have to come from us.

No one person has power on their own. Not even an absolute monarch or authoritarian dictator. Power is a group thing. No despot can put down a revolution if the security forces stay in their barracks or side with the people. No business survives if we stop buying its goods and services.

We're the ones with the real power - if only we'd realize it and act collectively

Any one of us can join in the capitalist game. All you need is an understanding of the mechanisms of wealth creation and the self-discipline to not spend all the money you earn on consumption.

But, if we're going to tackle the inequalities built into our economic and political systems, it's going to take more than individual conversions to capitalism. What's needed is a revolution, not so much in the streets, though I suspect there will be a role for that, but in the way we're prepared to act to ensure a fair go for all.

What will it look like? I don't know for sure, but I suspect it will require the creation of new political parties and a reinvigorated labour movement. It will require people demanding justice for all and not just for the privileged few. And, it's going to require a willingness for individuals to speak truth to power and demand political accountability.

The one thing I know for sure is, it's going to require political activism by a lot more of us. The 10 percent only get away with what they're doing because we let them. We don't ask questions. We believe what the media's talking heads tell us. We tolerate politicians that lie and bosses that exploit us.

The only way to change the dynamics of the game where you are is to get involved. What you do is up to you - but don't expect things to change if you don't do anything different.

Normal is the problem

Black Lives Matter protests in all fifty states of the USA and around the world are telling us something.

Now, here's the question. What are they telling you?

If you think it's about law and order, you're not listening to the frequency being used by the collective consciousness. You're still listening to some right-wing, conservative channel calling for everything to go back to normal.

What the protesters are telling us is normal is the problem.

And, let's not fool ourselves into believing this is only about the USA.

This is a worldwide problem where normal is rooted in systemic injustice.

The Chinese Communist Party may be enjoying the opportunity of the moment to lampoon the USA, but their society is based on deep systemic injustices as well. Just ask anyone protesting in the streets of Hong Kong or serving time for speaking out in dissent.

In Australia, the country we locals call the lucky country, you're not so lucky if you're born into our indigenous population. You're more likely to have a life experience any African American could identify with.

If you have yet to grasp the nature of the problem - it's ruling class privilege.

In the Western World, that translates to white privilege. In India, it translates to Hindu privilege. In China, it translates to Han Chinese privilege. I could go on, but I'm sure you get the message: there is a ruling group in every nation on earth.

As Canada's Prime Minister told us at a recent press conference, where he struggled to find the words to express how he felt about Trump's response to the protests, most of us are blind to the problem.

We're blind to it because we're part of the ruling class - even if we hold no positions of power. We're the ones who have access to the good education, the high paying jobs, the health system, and the decent housing. We're the ones the police protect.

The protests are not going to solve the problem and the problem won't go away when we go back to what we call normal.

It's not going to go away until we address the core issues underpinning the structural systemic injustice in our societies.

Seeing Things Differently

We are the ones who have to demand change and act to hold our politicians accountable. We need to exercise our right to vote and elect politicians who will represent the people instead of corporate wealth. And protest when they don't.

We are the ones who have to say it's not okay for the few to live in obscene luxury while so many of our fellow citizens of color live in poverty - even though they have full time jobs.

We are the ones that must demand changes to taxation and labour laws. We are the ones that have to demand better access to education, housing and health services for all.

And, we need to be prepared to share the benefits of citizenship with everyone in our society, regardless of color, race, or creed.

We need to open our eyes and our hearts.

We cannot go back to normal because normal is the problem.

Be warned. This is not going to be easy. We only have to look to Syria and China for reminders of what ruling elites will do to hang on to power.

And, disturbingly, while the BLM protesters were in the streets we saw the so-called leader of the free world threaten to do the same. Thankfully, he lost the 2020 election.

Disarming the police

Rethinking policing in light of recent events.

Too often, from my perspective, we've seen video coverage of armed police in the USA doing things we'd rather not have witnessed. I, for one, do not want to see that level of police arrogance and brutality in my community.

Given recent events closer to home, including the black lives matter protests, the police shooting of a man armed with a knife on a highway outside Melbourne, and the assault on an indigenous youth by a policeman in Sydney, I think we may have reached a moment, an inflection point, if you like, where we need to ask whether we want to continue consenting to having armed police on the streets of our communities.

In the United Kingdom, for example, police officers do not carry firearms unless the situation they expect to meet warrants it. In Australia, police wear personal sidearms at all times. In both countries, officers can call on more heavily

Seeing Things Differently

armed colleagues in those infrequent moments when the need arises.

Australia, unlike the USA, does not have a gun culture. People do not walk around with guns here. Most of us do not own or wish to own a firearm. But, it seems we have adopted American policing ideas when it comes to arming and clothing our police forces, instead of following the UK model. I find this disturbing, as American policing appears to be based on confrontation and the application of lethal force.

The problem, as I see it, is when you give a person a firearm, using it becomes an option and possessing it influences the holder's attitude and sense of invulnerability. None of those outcomes is positive.

I want the officer dealing with me to know his authority comes from his badge, not from his weapon.

I don't have a problem with police being armed when they are dealing with armed offenders. The UK model shows us that works. I do, however, have a problem when the person they are dealing with is someone armed with a knife having a mental health issue and they shoot him dead, despite outnumbering him five to one. That is not an acceptable outcome in the community I want to live in.

If police weren't armed for routine patrol work, they'd need to be trained to de-escalate confrontations and to use non-lethal forms of self-defence.

It's too easy and too deadly to simply pull out your revolver and shoot.

If you don't have that option, you have to think of something else, and you have to be trained to do that instead of being trained to hit your target in the chest.

And, what about community events? Why do the police supervising peaceful protests or attending the football need to be armed? Why do the police walking through our shopping centres or visiting our schools need to be armed?

We don't drive around with weapons in our cars, so why are the officers booking us for traffic infringements armed? It doesn't make sense. It's never made sense.

Police officers may claim they feel safer when they're armed all the time. I'm not sure I know what they're afraid of as Australia is not a violent society. What I do know is, I don't feel safer. And, you can bet your bottom dollar no indigenous Australian feels any safer because the police are armed.

I suspect arming the police was a fear tactic employed by law and order politicians wanting to impose order, without addressing the underlying social issues that lead to the criminal behaviour associated with poverty and injustice. We need to question the decisions of past politicians and demand change from the current crop claiming to represent our interests.

Australia is a safe place to live for most of us but it would be safer, especially for indigenous communities and people with mental health issues, if we disarmed our police and worked to address those issues that result in people living in poverty and injustice.

Transformation - not destruction

> *If you're out in the streets protesting, it's important to know where you think you're taking society.*

It doesn't take me to tell you there are a lot of things wrong with society. If you're protesting, you already know that. I'm not going to argue with your understanding.

There is no denying the existence of things like social injustice, systemic racial discrimination, inequitable distribution of resources, corruption, greed, abuse of power, and warmongering.

But, before you proceed with destroying everything in the name of social justice and racial equality, let's pause for a moment and see if there's anything good about the way society works.

Let's start with the big one: the police

We've had calls to both defund and disband the police. Disbanding is a form of what I understand as destruction.

Defunding, on the other hand, could lead to transformation - a change for the better.

In some parts of the world, we are dealing with corrupt, incompetent, and brutal police forces. But, in many towns and cities, we have honest, highly trained, competent, and trusted police forces. We need more of the latter and less of the former.

It's easy to call for the disbanding of the police in times like these, when we've seen or experienced expressions of police brutality in the name of law and order. However, we need to remember there are reasons why we created police forces in the first place and, as far as I can tell, those reasons are still with us - there are still some people who do not want to play by the rules, and shit happens.

In fact, most of the time, we live in safer societies because we have police. What we don't want is a police force drunk on its own power and lack of accountability. We don't want poorly trained and poorly paid police either, because, too often, such officers tend to embrace corruption and fail to act in accordance with set standards of behaviour.

We want police officers who know their job, have been trained properly, get paid appropriately, and who are committed to protecting their community.

In democracies, holding the police accountable comes back to us. We elect and pay the politicians and officials who are supposed to hold the police accountable. We're the people that let our politicians and officials get away with turning a blind eye to abuses of power. We are the ones who have to

Seeing Things Differently

stand up and hold our elected officials accountable for their failure to hold our police accountable.

It shouldn't have to fall to a teenager with a smartphone taking a video of a police officer committing a crime in broad daylight for us to act.

It's not just the lack of accountability for criminal acts committed by police that needs to be addressed. We need to review what we expect of our police and the tools we give them to work with. We want police to protect and secure our communities.

I know we don't need a paramilitary force armed to the teeth to do that in my local community, and I suspect you don't need one where you live either.

Transformation may require defunding, retraining or replacing existing officers, and disarming forces. Simply disbanding or destroying your police force is not the answer. You need to transform it into the force you want.

The United States, where this question has recently come into sharp focus, has a unique challenge in relation to transforming its policing. The USA has 50 states and 14 territories but it has close to 18,000 police forces. Basically, every state, county, and city has its own police force, and then there's the FBI.

New York State, for example, with an estimated population of 19.4 million, has over 500 law enforcement agencies

A country like Australia, also a federation, has 6 states and 9 territories but it only has 6 state police forces, 1 territory police force, and 1 federal police force - that's a total of 8 police forces for an estimated national population of 25.5 million.

In the USA, a transformation of policing might require a massive reduction in the number of police forces as they come to terms with what sort of society they want to live in.

Now, let's look at capitalism.

In the West, we live in what we call liberal democracies with capitalist economies, where capitalism has become a dirty word for describing the system used by the wealthy to screw the rest of us.

In fact, it's become fashionable to blame capitalism for many of our social and environmental problems, and there is, no doubt, some truth behind those claims. But, do we want to see the destruction or transformation of capitalism?

There must be something to capitalism that makes it attractive, seeing that China embraced it to successfully improve the standard of living of millions of people - following the disasters of Mao's version of Marxist-Leninism.

There is no doubt capitalism in the West is in need of transformation.

Modern capitalism lost its way when the focus shifted to maximising shareholder profits at the expense of everything else. In case you missed it, the problem is not the system *per se* but the driving motivation of the operators of the corporate world. It's the shortsighted self-interest of the few that's blinding us to the benefits of capitalism.

Seeing Things Differently

There is another form capitalism could take: stakeholder or conscious capitalism.

This form of capitalism takes into account the interests of all stakeholders involved in an enterprise: customers, suppliers, employees, shareholders and local communities. This is a form of capitalism that does not seek to exploit any of its stakeholders or avoid paying the taxes needed to support its local community.

If it comes to a choice between destroying or transforming the system to address questions of social and economic equity, I'm for transformation.

Destruction is not necessary when a workable alternative exists - an alternative that only requires a resetting of priorities from self-interest to community interest.

We can do this. All it requires is acting together for our common good.

We are not a society of entrepreneurs

Questioning the role of the billionaire dream in an equitable society.

Capitalist economies enable entrepreneurs - people with big ideas and the drive to start a business. We've all heard of successful entrepreneurs, people like Jeff Bezos (Amazon), Bill Gates (Microsoft), and Steve Jobs (Apple), who took an idea and turned it into a successful business.

Their stories inspire us to create and build businesses. And, if their stories are not enough, there are plenty of people selling us the dream of entrepreneurship - tempting us to give up our jobs and start a business. But, you might want to consider a few things before you follow their advice and take that leap.

Looking behind the dazzle of the billionaire dream

No one person builds a successful business. Building a business is a team effort. The initiating spark and drive may come from one inspired person, but the capital, skills, and effort mostly come from other people.

Building a business is a risky venture. There is no guarantee you will succeed, no matter how good your idea is, and the failure rate is high. Most of us are risk adverse, and those who take the plunge to birth a business often do so with other people's money.

In fact, there's an industry devoted to funding other people's dreams: venture capital. The aim of venture capitalists is to profit from underwriting the risk of developing a new idea or launching a product or service - but they don't just fund anybody who comes along with an idea and they always want equity in your venture.

It doesn't matter how talented you are either, unless you're going to be happy as a one person business, like many creatives. There is only so much an individual can achieve.

Jeff Bezos, for example, started as a garage-based entrepreneur with a small number of employees but Amazon now employs hundreds of thousands of people in its worldwide operation. That's quite a team and it has to be managed.

Entrepreneurs need people, and not only to build and operate their businesses. They need people to buy their products or services, and they rely upon services provided by other businesses and government - services that depend upon the willingness of people to engage in employment.

The role of employees

This is where most of us come in. We're the employees, the people that make things happen, the people that enable businesses to succeed.

You do not need to embrace the entrepreneurial dream to be successful. You can be successful as an employee simply by being good at your job. You can attain financial independence by investing in other people's businesses. You don't have to start one of your own.

The challenge, though, is to find ways to more equitably reward those of us who serve, so we can invest to secure our financial futures, instead of allowing the system to continue to make billionaires at our expense.

If we don't address this challenge, there's likely to be more protests in the streets as people demand their fair share. And, if you think that's unlikely, you might want to research the French Revolution.

Essential workers

If we've learnt anything from the Covid pandemic, it's that essential workers are more important than entrepreneurs. The economy may reward the risk takers under normal circumstances, but society always needs the service of those willing to serve regardless of the circumstances.

Seeing Things Differently

We will always need essential workers to look after people's health and keep the economy going so we can eat, flush the toilet, and turn on the lights. We need to look after our essential workers and stop taking them for granted.

There is no point in becoming the next billionaire if nothing works and there's no-one there to fix it.

Transparency brings everything into the light of day

Closed doors are being opened before our eyes.

Transparency leads to change in individuals, institutions, and societies.

Transparency exposes things. It's uncomfortable for individuals. It shines a light on dubious dealings within institutions, dealings the powerful would prefer we mere mortals knew nothing about. It leads to revolutions where the people decide to challenge the status quo in society.

Personal transparency

Transparency at the personal level involves working with your shadow. In other words, it means confronting those aspects of yourself you don't want to admit to - all those parts of yourself you want to keep hidden from yourself and from others.

You are transformed by integrating your shadow into your wholeness. You grow by coming to terms with the truth that we are all shades of grey. None of us are all light or all dark.

The benefit of that integration is you can stop pretending and start being authentic. You can be who you really are instead of hiding behind a socially acceptable mask.

Institutional transparency

Transparency at the institutional level usually involves public exposure of misbehaviour, especially when institutions hold dark secrets. Often, somebody within the institution has to blow the whistle on corrupt behaviour before we conduct some type of inquiry or investigation to expose that behaviour and force change. Many times, we're up against vested interests that want to keep things the way they are.

In Australia, we call these transformational investigations Royal Commissions. We've recently had Royal Commissions into:

- Institutional Responses to Child Sexual Abuse, and
- Misconduct in the Banking, Superannuation and Financial Services Industry

Both these investigations exposed egregious behaviour by the institutions involved. And, what's worse, these institutions are the very ones that, not so long ago, we trusted. Those institutions are now grappling with their public shaming and mandated changes.

In the United States of America, we've witnessed the uncovering of egregious political behaviour and the impeachment of a sitting president. Whatever you think of Trump, his behaviour has shone a spotlight on the workings of the American Congress and the lengths to which some members of the Republican Party will go to defend the apparently indefensible.

But, it's not only the USA where we're seeing things in turmoil. There have been people in the streets in Chile, Ecuador, Hong Kong, Iraq, and Lebanon - to name a few places that have made the news - demanding an end to corrupt government and inequality.

In Bolivia, the security forces sided with the people and the President resigned. Unfortunately, in most places the security forces and other paramilitary groups side with the government and people are killed for protesting.

Something is going on. It's not just people demanding action on corruption and inequality. We also have millions of people across the globe protesting governments' inaction on addressing global warming and climate change.

A few years ago I read *Transparency* by Penney Pierce, in which she introduced the idea of entering an age in which everything hidden will be exposed.

It seems the more awake people become, the more transparent the workings of the world become - and that leads to action.

I think Penney might have been on the money.

A note from Peter

If you found the material in ***Seeing Things Differently*** helpful and informative, you can help other readers discover the book by telling them about your experience through writing a review.

If you're interested, you can find more of my articles on www.medium.com/@petermulraney and details about my books on www.petermulraney.com

Thanks for taking the time to read ***Seeing Things Differently.*** I hope you found the material engaging enough to start rethinking what you've been told about how the world works, and to start taking a greater interest in what's going on in your world.

Also by Peter Mulraney

Writings of the Mystic

Sharing the Journey: Reflections of a Reluctant Mystic
My Life is My Responsibility: Insights for Conscious Living
I Am Affirmations: The Power of Words
Beyond the Words: Reflections on I Am Affirmations
Mystical Journey: A Handbook for Modern Mystics
Making Space for the Divine

Sharing the Journey Coloring Books
Mandalas
Mandalas by 3

Sharing the Journey Coloring Journals
Sharing the Journey Coloring Journal
Sharing the Journey Coloring Journal ~Discovery
Sharing the Journey Coloring Journal ~ Reflection

Crime Fiction

Travers and Palumbo series
Desolation
Distraction

Inspector West series

After

The Holiday

Holy Death

Whistleblower

Twisted Justice

The East Park Syndicate

Inspector West Collection One

Inspector West Collection Two

Stella Bruno Investigates series

The Identity Thief

A Gun of Many Parts

Bones in the Forest

A Deadly Game of Hangman

Taken

Fallout

The Melrose Case

The Scam

Deception

Stella Bruno Investigates: Books 1 to 6

The Identity Thief Collection

The Fallout Collection

The Deception Collection

Ryan Holiday PI Short Stories

Rosie

Framed

Other Fiction

The New Girlfriend

Self-Help

Living Alone series
After She's Gone

Cooking 4 One

Sanity Savers

Living Alone (Collection)

Living Alone Journal

Everyday Business Skills
Everyday Project Management

Everyday Productivity

Everyday Money Management